MW00806891

PRAISE FOR NANCY GEENEN AND

The Advantage *of* Other

"Good leaders provide direction, purpose, and reason for a group or organization to follow. They also share their knowledge, wisdom, and experience with others. Their leadership becomes a calling to serve others. Nancy Geenen is a leader who has risen to the top of her field and industry because she builds teams that put people first and recognize the importance of equity and inclusion. Her stories and recommendations for entrepreneurs in *The Advantage of Others* are clear, specific, and on target in today's business and social climate."

—Lynda Applegate

Baker Foundation Professor, Sarofim-Rock Professor of Business Administration, Emerita

"As Geenen says, employees (the people) are a competitive advantage, and whether a business leader is searching for new talent or new customers, diversity in leadership is a significant consideration. *The Advantage of Other* is a relatable read that reminds us of that in a unique and fresh manner. I found her book engaging and valuable and will recommend that my business students—future leaders—read it."

—Tanya Hubanks, JD, SHRM-SCP

"Read, discuss, apply, and share *The Advantage of Other*. Embracing the message of this timely book will add value to your business and your life. Nancy Geenen nails the critical gaps between leadership and management for women owned and led businesses. This is the book that will guide your leadership and the commitment to scaling your business; it will have you racing into the world to _ become a company of purpose on your path to personal and professional success."

—Edie Fraser

CEO, WBC; Founder of Diversity Best Practices and STEMconnector

"Nancy Geenen shows up! In *The Advantage of Other*, Nancy details a plan for business leaders to make a difference. She is a storyteller that imbeds life learnings while inspiring us to challenge the status quo. A teacher, coach, mentor, and friend, Nancy leads with her heart."

— Julie Castro Abrams

Founder and CEO, How Women Lead, Managing Partner, How Women Invest

"Nancy is the consummate talent to meet customers where they are and to move them forward. She is brave enough to take on new opportunities and help customers build solutions that work for them. Through her focused quietness she allows everyone to think, learn, grow, and succeed."

—Sandra Eberhard

President and CEO, Women's Business Economic Council (WBEC) Metro NY and DMV

"I've attended many presentations, workshops, and events on diversity, equity, and inclusion (DEI). I've read multiple articles, blogs, and papers. I can say, without a doubt, that Geenen's *The Advantage of Other* drew me in like others hadn't. Maybe it is because of her self-professed 'unique ability to teach.' Maybe it is because she is an exceptional storyteller. Maybe it is because her prose is personable, relatable, authentic, and humble. Maybe it is because she uses her legal training to effectively present recommendations that guide implementation of each of the DEI concepts she presents. Or, likely, it is because of all of these.

"Geenen likes alliteration, and each chapter in *The Advantage of Other* presents business leaders with a guide to creating a culture of inclusivity via the Ps. The foundation of developing a supporting work environment is set in chapter one via the power of story—Geenen uses her story and encourages the readers to consider theirs. The next chapters explore the five pillars of an organization (people, presence, pipeline, partners, and profits). Throughout, she explains DEI concepts in an easy to understand manner, differentiating between managing and leading, helping the reader to be a better version of their self in ways that promote inclusivity—to be curious and to keep learning.

"I have had the distinct honor of working with Nancy Geenen since 2021, volunteering on the Board of Directors for the Golden Gate Business Association in San Francisco. I have seen first-hand that DEI runs through Nancy's veins. I am constantly amazed by Nancy's passion and drive for equity and inclusion. The drive and passion make *The Advantage of Other* an essential book for any C-suite executive and business owners. In *The Advantage of Other*, Nancy shows the reader how equity and inclusion begin with trust and, more importantly, how to apply this concept to become an exceptional leader."

—Tony Archuleta-Perkins, MBA, MS
Volunteer President of the Golden Gate Business Association

"Nancy Geenen gets it. She's authored the definitive playbook for leading in a modern, post-pandemic world, powered by a DEI framework. Nancy nails the current realities of leading with head and heart, where the bottom line is equally important as how you get there. Leaders who pay attention to *The Advantage of Other* will have the edge as we face the new post-pandemic era. Nancy Geenen provides a simple playbook to help leaders navigate the peaks and valleys of the modern workforce, where belonging and engagement drive performance and lead to success. This is a must-read for any entrepreneur and leadership team. With *Advantage of Other*, Nancy Geenen offers leaders an essential and heartfelt framework for equitable and inclusive leadership that drives results. You may see yourself in these pages."

—Ryan Wines
Founder and CEO, Marmoset

"*The Advantage of Other* offers a fresh perspective on leading in today's world. Nancy Geenen speaks from experience, offering a path of inclusivity and belonging for all. Expanding our leadership lens means being active learners willing to show our vulnerability while elevating the teams we serve. This book offers a path to Intentional Greatness® while doing exactly that!"

—Sue Hawkes
Best Selling Author, Expert EOS® Implementer, Speaker

"I have had the honor and privilege to not only work with Nancy Geenen, but also come to know her as a friend and peer. *The Advantage of Other* uses the power of story, vulnerability, and transparency to share, highlight, and teach leaders how we can create awesome teams through DEI. In working with Nancy, she has enabled my team to go further together. And I encourage you to pick up this book and bring others on the journey. It will bring us all to a greater good."

—Michele Bailey
Forbes author of Gratitude

"For those leaders passionate about creating a culture of mattering and belonging there is no better resource than *The Advantage of Other*. By sharing vulnerable and relatable stories Nancy serves as your navigator toward true understanding and awareness of the challenges that exist within the workplace. Practical tools provided support diversity, equity, and inclusion within business, and more importantly, our world. Having personal, real world experience working with

Nancy and her Flexability team, we've benefitted from her wisdom to build the most high-performing teams that serve the greater good. Through *The Advantage of Other*, it's now available to everyone!"

—Kelly Knight
President & Integrator, EOS Worldwide

The Advantage of Other

Stay curious!

— Mary

NANCY GEENEN

The Advantage *of* Other

A Leader's Guide to Building an Equitable, Dynamic, and Productive Workplace

Advantage | Books

Published by Advantage, Charleston, South Carolina.
Member of Advantage Media.

ADVANTAGE is a registered trademark, and the Advantage colophon is a trademark of Advantage Media Group, Inc.

Printed in the United States of America.

10 9 8 7 6 5 4 3 2 1

ISBN: 978-1-64225-377-1 (Hardcover)
ISBN: 978-1-64225-461-7 (eBook)

LCCN: 2023900199

Cover design by Danna Steele.
Layout design by Analisa Smith.

This publication is designed to provide accurate and authoritative information in regard to the subject matter covered. It is sold with the understanding that the publisher is not engaged in rendering legal, accounting, or other professional services. If legal advice or other expert assistance is required, the services of a competent professional person should be sought.

Advantage Media helps busy entrepreneurs, CEOs, and leaders write and publish a book to grow their business and become the authority in their field. Advantage authors comprise an exclusive community of industry professionals, idea-makers, and thought leaders. Do you have a book idea or manuscript for consideration? We would love to hear from you at **AdvantageMedia.com**.

To Judith, Lucy, and Joy ...
because you showed me that I belong.

CONTENTS

INTRODUCTION

You're not a great leader until you grow a
leader who grows another leader.
—SUE HAWKES

People, our employees, are *the* competitive advantage in our businesses.

This is a book designed to support business leaders who are committed to diversity, equity, and inclusion in the workplace. As leaders, we must unlearn some old habits and replace those with new practices that become habits over time. Here's an easy one: refer to your employees as *team members*.

Diversity is the representation of many identities and lived experiences. Stated another way, it's who is invited into the room.

Equity is the access to career opportunities, resources, and tools needed to thrive uniquely in the workplace.

Inclusion is the IMPACT on the team member that lets her trust that she is both seen and heard and heard because she is seen.

1

An inclusive leader values others' perspectives and creates belonging. This leader creates a high-trust environment where everyone at the table knows their ideas are respected and given the consideration as if they were the most important person in the room. Inclusion is often the determining factor as to whether top talent remains and thrives. The growth trajectory of any business is dependent on finding, training, and retaining the best talent available with actionable and sustainable strategies. There is not a one-and-done fix.

Mattering and *belonging* are really two separate ideas. Mattering is about sponsorship of others, seeking out opportunities, making introductions and checking in, intentionally and continuously. Belonging is about those everyday roundtable discussions to which we add our voices because our opinions, ideas, and recommendations are valued. Creating a culture of mattering and belonging requires awareness, practice, and vigilance.

Recent diversity research and data are conclusive: Firms with diverse leadership teams are 45 percent more likely to report growth due to innovation.[1] Further, the same study found that 70 percent of these diverse leadership teams reported that these teams developed new and innovative products to better serve their team members and customers. Follow-on studies expanded the research and data. Teams with gender or disability diversity reported 25 percent better performance than their peers.[2] Teams with racial or ethnic diversity

---

1   Sylvia Ann Hewlett, Melinda Marshall, and Laura Sherbin, "How Diversity Can Drive Innovation," Harvard Business Review, December 2013, https://hbr.org/2013/12/how-diversity-can-drive-innovation; Rocio Lorenzo and Martin Reeves, "How and Where Diversity Drives Financial Performance," Harvard Business Review, January 30, 2018, https://hbr.org/2018/01/how-and-where-diversity-drives-financial-performance.

2   Vivian Hunt, Dennis Layon, Sara Prince, "Diversity Matters," McKinsey & Company, February 2, 2015; Vivian Hunt, Sara Prince, Kevin Dolan, Sundiatu Dixon-Fyle, "Diversity Wins," McKinsey & Company, May 2020.

reported 36 percent better performance.[3] Overall, diverse teams were found to be 87 percent better decision makers than nondiverse teams.[4] According to the most recent census data, 67 percent of the US workforce is between the ages of twenty-one and fifty-two and is more diverse than any other prior generation.[5] Sixty percent of millennials, Gen Yers, and Gen Xers think it's important to support brands that have diverse leadership and that invest in social causes.[6] Whether the business leader is looking for talent or new customers, diversity in leadership is a significant consideration.

For the business leader, the combination of innovation and performance data is a key to achieving results in the workplace and the marketplace. Being open to diverse voices and lived experiences encourages the team to approach problem-solving and innovation from all points of the compass. This openness at the leadership level encourages the rest of the organization to break through barriers that keep the business from achieving the vision and mission.

Curiosity and listening are the tools that drive inclusivity—decreasing self-centeredness and increasing the capacity to hear different stories, different experiences, and different perspectives that challenge the status quo. Strong leadership values many, sometimes conflicting, perspectives. Many of us know the advice: you can't keep doing the same things and expect different results. As leaders, we must invite and inspire a willingness to speak up and step up. It's a matter of creating the space for yourself and your team members to

---

3   Hunt, Prince, Dolan, and Dixon-Fyle, "Diversity Wins"; Vivian Hunt, Sara Prince, Sundiatu Dixon-Fyle, Larina Yee, "Delivering through Diversity," McKinsey & Company, January 2018.

4   Hunt, Prince, Dolan, and Dixon-Fyle, "Diversity Wins."

5   Hunt, Prince, Dolan, and Dixon-Fyle, "Diversity Wins"; Janie Boschma et al., "Census Release Shows America Is More Diverse and Multiracial than Ever," CNN Money, updated August 12, 2021.

6   Boschma et al., "Census Release."

be curious, to think expansively, and to learn so that everyone knows they are expected to contribute.

Accountability and execution are the tools that drive an equitable workplace—investing in the infrastructure of the business that affects the stakeholders the most. Providing the "right" resources and opportunities for everyone in the workplace from the stockroom to the boardroom is the key to equity. Often, I ask leaders who is the most important person in the company. Many times, I hear that it is the leader setting the vision and the strategy, and then the employees who are executing the strategy. Sometimes, I hear the response that it is the employee who is engaging with the customer. Rarely do I hear that it is the leader who is prioritizing the growth and well-being of the team. There's a chain reaction, essentially a cause and effect at work. If the leader connects and builds trust with the teams, then the teams build trust with and among each other, rewarding the customer with similar treatment. In this way, leaders build loyalty with team members who, in turn, build loyal relationships with customers, who then become advocates for the brand.

This book is a guide for self-exploration for a leader who wants to create a culture of inclusivity to build high-performing teams within the company. The chapters focus on the five pillars of an organization: *people, presence, pipeline, partners*, and *profits*. Yes, I do like alliteration. I start with a story, an anecdote or vignette, that sets up the learnings for the reader. I discuss the goals and objectives that a business should hope to achieve in each area. For example, presence covers a leader's personal brand within the company. Each chapter concludes with recommendations to guide implementation of one or more concepts from the chapter. I invite you as the leader to experience this journey from both my and your own perspective.

The best leaders recognize there is a difference between leading and managing. Leading is a way of *being* accountable to oneself and the team. Managing is a way of *holding* the team accountable to each other. We've got to create a leadership culture of mattering and belonging in business for both short- and long-term sustainability and growth.

CHAPTER 1

The Power of Story

Learn to be still in the midst of activity and vibrantly alive in repose.
—INDIRA GANDHI

I want to invite you to start at the beginning with me. Before we discuss the broader ideas of diversity, equity, and inclusion at work; long before we discuss how to create a supportive work environment for all people; and long, long before we address specific workplace policies like the use of pronouns in the workplace, I invite you to get curious, to approach this book with the wonder of a child. To be childlike is to ask questions and to learn new skills, all while being secure in the space of not knowing. Beginners aren't worried about getting it right—not the first time, or the second time, or even the time after that. If you choose to live and work with a beginner's mindset, then the process of mastery, the attention that you give to that journey, becomes enjoyable.

A rabbi I knew was fond of saying "It's never too late, but it's later than you think." You have picked up this book for a reason (or maybe many reasons), right here, right now. Perhaps it was a curiosity about the title, or yearning for the "right way" to create a DEI program at work, or caring for your employees through self-improvement as a leader, or even building trust with your team. It's a perfect time to begin your journey, because now is better than later, and perfection is an illusion. Adopt the mantra: progress, not perfection.

The path to leadership has many, many steps, and to master something requires consistent intention and attention. Along the way, sometimes you'll go three steps forward, only to fall two steps back. Sometimes you'll get knocked down completely, and it will take great effort to get back up. Mastery is the journey in between failure and perfection "because both are merely inaccurate labels of a moment in time."[7] Enjoy that space in between, and remember that there is enough room for all of us.

Think of this journey like a backyard garden. If you plant the seeds in the ground immediately, they may get swept away by rain or eaten by animals. If you start the seeds indoors on your counter space—a protected environment—the seedlings turn to shoots and will be ready to be planted in the open where they will be hearty enough to survive the immediate challenges of the environment. Of course, that doesn't mean that the job is done! These plants require attention and the right resources—water, soil, the right amount of sunlight or shade. If you take care and pay attention as you introduce new challenges, bit by bit, there's a higher likelihood that your little seedlings will grow and thrive. The guardian of this garden must enjoy the process and be intentional in the journey. To paraphrase the quote by Indira Gandhi: Be willing to sit quietly amid the discomfort of not

---

7   Brené Brown, Atlas of the Heart (New York: Penguin Random House, November 30, 2021).

knowing the right answer, and take time to reflect, see things clearly, and restore yourself.

Begin with Your Story

We all have a story to tell. More importantly, reexamine the stories that you have always told yourself, and dive deeper into the truths that these stories hold. When we share our stories, we see the similarities, and the differences, among us, and from there, we can discover how to learn from one another and from one another's stories.

I believe that sharing your story is one of the best ways to create and build trust. Telling your story is hard work because it doesn't always feel like it matters, or that it is useful to others. The resistance I feel is real. Yet I know that my story matters and that I belong. When I know that I matter and I belong, I'm at my best. I'm able to be a thoughtful leader who listens with all my senses, so that my team knows they also matter and belong. Though, I must admit, even now, after years of doing this work, the vulnerability required to share my story makes me nervous. With this in mind, I will tell you a little bit more about myself, where I come from, and how I arrived here, as the CEO of Flexability, a social impact firm that focuses on equity and inclusion in the workplace.

The Early Years

I went to a very small high school in Wisconsin whose motto was "Remember who you are and what you represent." I loved my school—my mother taught there, my two brothers and my sister went there—and I very much took that school motto to heart. In addition to having the very best grades, I was a High School All-American in both tennis and basketball. I was proving that I belonged, always searching for acceptance through excellence. And although I didn't have many friends (as I had little time for the social life of a normal high school student,) I was determined to represent my school, my family, and my community well.

There was only one small issue.

In the 1970s, no one used the word "lesbian." Or, if they did, it was said in hushed tones, certainly not meant as a compliment, and no one dared say it directly to my face. Looking back, I can see that my parents and a few of my teachers knew my secret, but whenever anyone tried to broach the subject with me, even in a loving and supportive way, I was so scared of rejection that I cut off all efforts. Fear showed up as anger. I couldn't hear their concern over that little voice in my head that said "Get straight As, be a great athlete, represent the colors of your team, make your parents proud, and remember that it's always about the greater good." I was sure that if anyone knew the truth, I would become unlovable and no longer part of the team.

I was sure that if anyone knew the truth, I would become unlovable and no longer part of the team.

In Wisconsin, I used a fake ID to hide my identity at the local gay bar. The place was a little scary—and a lot seedy. I didn't drink; I would just go to dance and to be with "others" like me. If this was the club that would include me, I wasn't sure I wanted to be a member. And with my fake ID in hand, no one ever knew my name or where I came from. I acquired the nickname "California." I was a chameleon, becoming whatever other people wanted me to be, even in the spaces where I might be myself. Always looking for that place to belong, I never quite fit in.

Finding My Footing

At Stanford, in the late seventies and early eighties, there was just LG, not LGBTQIA (lesbian, gay, bisexual, transgender, queer and/or questioning, intersex, asexual and ally). PFLAG (Parents and Friends of Lesbians and Gays), the first organization dedicated to supporting the gay community in their relationships with straight friends and family members, wasn't even a decade old. Women athletes were just starting to see the benefits of Title IX. What we did have, however, were words like "queer," "dyke," and "butch," and they were all words meant to cause harm. Even to this day, I can't hear the word "queer" without a trigger reaction, even though I know that younger generations have reclaimed this word as a label of empowerment.

College was also the time when I went from being an exceptional student to an average student among the exceptional students. The fact that I graduated in four years seems like a miracle. It wasn't until I found my way to the English department, with a great advisor, who was, incidentally, also gay, that I found my footing in college. He was an authority in Shakespearean theater, and he taught me how to "play a role." He explained how to be the person that people needed me to be on the surface, so I could stay private and protected on the inside. My chameleon skills grew stronger. While this certainly isn't the advice that I would offer any young person now, I know his advice was intended to shield and protect my otherness from harm.

While I let go of my idea of myself as an exceptional student, I also had to release the idea of myself as an exceptional athlete as well. While playing soccer for Stanford during my first year, I was tackled violently by a goalie from a rival school. She hit me so hard that I lifted into the air, did a full flip and a half, and landed hard on the bottom half of my left leg. The upper and lower parts of my knee just split apart, yanking the knee out of its socket and tearing most of the cartilage. Even with a "bad wheel," I continued to play for Stanford throughout my college career, lettering in both field hockey and basketball. To keep that connection to my teammates and coaches, I gave up on most of the required rehabilitation and forged ahead.

During these years of bench sitting, I watched and learned from my coaches: how they developed individuals, tested strategies, developed team skills, and encouraged every player regardless of her star power. These coaches focused on accountability and common goals to forge a winning attitude and produce results. Every time I put on that big ugly brace (which isn't very often these days), I remember what it felt like to matter and belong, even when I could barely run. I was part of the team; my contributions were valued.

I wish I could say I had come to love and accept myself during my college years, but unfortunately, the path toward self-love and acceptance is never quite a "straight" line. Stanford was a great place to grow and work on some of my anger issues. I found an identity within a community of women, athletes, and supportive professors. But there were still a lot of emotional issues I refused to address. I stayed on at Stanford and earned my master's degree in education (with much better grades) and a lifetime teaching credential.

I think it's important to note that everyone has some version of the "I never quite fit in in high school." No matter if you were a jock, a drama kid, a nerd, a richie-rich or a kid in a single-family home, everyone feels like an outsider at some point in their childhood and adolescence. We were all doing our best to get along. The details are different, but the feelings of otherness are very similar. I consider myself very fortunate that, despite my differences, I enjoyed the privilege of financial security, as well as support from my family and community. I only wish I had understood that I did matter and that

I did belong, to accept the love and commitment offered to me by my family much earlier in my life.

Gaining Skills and Experience

My first job was teaching at a coed Catholic high school in the San Francisco Bay Area. By day, I was an English teacher and tennis coach, and by night, I was living in East Palo Alto, in an apartment above a bunch of hippies who sold psychedelic mushrooms for a living. Every morning I'd ride my motorcycle to work and change into my uniform on campus—a button-down collared shirt with a sweater vest, chino slacks, and penny loafers. My chameleon skills helped me to blend in wherever I went.

I think back on this time as a period in my life when I really began to figure myself out. Partially, I credit this to working with a diverse student population. There were, on average, forty kids in each classroom, and very few of those kids were planning to go to a four-year college or university. Most students were planning to go to a vocational school, a community college, or the military. As I was only four or five years older than many of these students, it often felt like I had been given an opportunity to "repeat" high school and to do some self-reflection using the stories of my students. I thought about how I would do it differently and the experiences I could share.

Teaching is my unique ability. I loved teaching and coaching. I taught Shakespeare and science fiction to seniors, literature and writing to sophomores and juniors, and one period of physical education each day. It was an opportunity to combine the wisdom and advice I had garnered over the years—from my parents, my coaches, my college advisor—and share it through literature. I got a kick out of being called Ms. Geenen, as I was still a kid myself. I brought my childlike curiosity to the job, learning in real time what worked and what didn't. I made lots of mistakes, but I also wasn't afraid to own those mistakes when I made them, which I think was a new and welcome approach from an authority figure for most of those students. We had many do-overs in my classroom.

It's very possible that I would still be teaching today, had the athletic director, another mentor of mine at the time, not given me some tough love. "Look, you're clearly a great coach, and you're spectacular in the classroom. Who you are is really special, but it may get in the way of your teaching," she said one afternoon, taking me aside. As she said this, I was sure she was referring to my sexuality. "Now look at the rest of us. We're ten, fifteen, twenty years your senior. Is this where you want to be when you're forty? You have a real talent, and I think your community needs you. I think the world needs you."

These words weren't exactly easy to hear. *Am I being fired? Because I'm gay?* I had to admit, she had a point. I looked around at my coworkers, and they weren't like me. I was friends with a few, although we didn't socialize outside of work. The work of teaching was fulfilling, and yet many teachers complained about the job, not the work. Meanwhile, at the age of twenty-three, I was in more debt than I should have been, making only $11,000 a year and spending money like I was making much more.

The athletic director continued, "You've got to decide that you love this work enough to stay here. And as much as I'd love for you to stay, if you don't see yourself loving it for the next twenty years, you should really go and explore your options, so you can have a clear idea of what comes next." So I did what many of my friends did: I went to law school.

Proving Myself

My first summer of law school, I worked for the Legal Aid Society in San Mateo County in the elder care unit. Social security administrative hearings did not require advocates to be attorneys. I discovered that I was excellent at process, procedures, and debate. I loved that moment when I could see the dead-end of the argument of my opponent. I loved winning. With a good amount of guidance, I became the writer and director of my own production. Winning produced results for my elderly clients. I was advocating to get them the money and benefits they had earned.

Being a lawyer, it turned out, meant turning every page, looking under every rock, and converting my natural curiosity into true investigative skills. I also learned another valuable lesson at the time: truth is a variable of context. I was convinced that I was fighting for truth and justice. Many of my clients stretched the truth, a lot, to win. This was a shocking revelation to me, but it was also a bit of a comfort as well. After all, I wasn't exactly telling the truth about who I was either.

I got my first job out of law school clerking for a fancy law firm in San Francisco. The office had views of the San Francisco Bay on three sides. While I certainly had the credentials and the grades to get the job, in truth, I think that I got the job because I could fit in with the "locker room guys" in the litigation department. (Years later, when I had ascended the ranks and achieved a leadership position at this firm, I was able to go back and read all my reviews from that summer clerkship. It was clear that, while they were certainly interested in my potential as a lawyer, some of the "guys" were *more* interested in winning the summer softball league championship!)

I was "out" to a few colleagues at work, and I was still very much treated like "one of the guys." I played a reliable second base (even with my brace); I was a scratch golfer; I drank great cabernets and smoked cigars. I kept up with the best of them in conversations about wine, sports, or investing. For the first time in my life, all those interests I had developed on the porch talking with my father were finally paying off. I belonged. We never talked about my romantic relationships.

I was still using my chameleon skills to fit in and belong to the gang. I adjusted to become what everyone wanted me to be—my coworkers, my clients, and even the judges and the juries. Despite being treated like one of the guys, I still showed up to work each day in a little flouncy scarf, white and blue pinpoint collared shirts, and a suit jacket and skirt. I never dreamed of wearing pants to work. While I was doing my part to fit in, my mentor, MKM, was doing his part to make sure I knew I belonged. When a trash-hauling business client insisted that they wouldn't work with a woman, MKM refused to appease their demands by simply giving them a new lawyer. Instead, he stated, "Listen, this woman is the reason we're going to win, so if you don't want her on your team, you are decreasing your odds of winning." Not only did we win that case, but that case was the reason I made partner earlier than some of my law school classmates. After that case, the guys went to Las Vegas to celebrate the win with the client. Even though I was invited on the trip, I had no interest in the Las Vegas activities. Just being invited along was a clear indication to me that I mattered and belonged.

My relationship with MKM, both professional and personal, is one of the most meaningful of my professional career. MKM was a senior partner on the executive committee and headed up the litigation practice. Our offices were across the hall from one another, and he would often pop his head into my office to just chat or say hello. I appreciated his curiosity about what I was working on and his willingness to invite me to discuss issues in his cases. Early on,

MKM let me know he knew that I was gay, although he didn't use the word *lesbian*. We would spend late nights at the bar together: MKM telling me stories of Vietnam and me sharing stories of my college sports adventures.

As a naval aviator who had served in Vietnam, his greatest compliment to me was to call me his "Marine." While this may not mean much to some people, I knew that the Marines were the ones that got stuff done, no matter the personal cost or hardship. I stormed the beaches, cleared the fields, and paved the way for the rest of the team. "If it positively, absolutely has to be destroyed overnight, trust Geenen to get it done." We were always faithful to our mission (client) and never left anyone behind. At the time, I did not realize that this was my first training class on mattering and belonging.

MKM also brought process and discipline to our work. He taught me to work hard when I had to and to coast when I could. This meant that I should work hard and be present when I was on the job, and when I was out of the office, I should really disconnect. I saw how he would take two or three weeks away from work and would make no apologies about needing to unplug to recalibrate for the next case ahead of him. From his example, I learned to truly disconnect, go fishing, play golf, or travel for weeks at a time. I used the time to recover and recharge.

The other skill that I watched MKM model was the ability to review his work, to really evaluate—without ego or attachment—what worked and what didn't. It was his belief that, if you always have a system, then you can always go back and do it the same way and figure out why things worked out the way they did. Having a system allowed us to return to the strategy and say "OK, where did we deviate? What happened to us that we didn't anticipate?" I became fascinated by this loop of constant improvement that we called "After Action Reports," named very much in the style of a military operation.

Broadening My Horizons

Transitions are always difficult for me. At a time, when the leadership of the firm was in doubt, I got the heck out of town. It was my classic fight-or-flight response to conflict. I fled the country and took a legal job at the United Nations in Geneva, Switzerland. As much as I'd like to claim that I wanted to be shaken out of my comfort zone and forced to confront new ideas, the truth is I was scared. Although I had traveled extensively outside of the country before, I had never really considered living overseas.

For two years, my job was to prosecute the claims regarding infrastructure—roads, damns, bridges—arising from Iraq's unlawful invasion of Kuwait and the subsequent military conflict. The commissioners and UN governing council were completely different from what I had known in California. Although the Bay Area is a diverse city, in Geneva, these decision makers reflected the membership of the United Nations, intentionally made up of people from all over the world.

From the moment I arrived, it was clear there was a different way of being, doing, and thinking about leadership. For example, at the time, I was wearing a brace on my leg or walking with a cane. While in the United States, people would avert their gaze or make sure never to ask about my "injury/ability." At the UN, my colleagues were completely unabashed about drawing attention to it. There was a Polish woman who took to calling me the "Little Crippled Girl," and the name stuck. She told me she had trouble remembering my name, and if she mentioned the brace, people knew who she was talking about. I didn't take offense. I understood that she wasn't trying to be mean. She asked about my brace and created a hero story about my soccer career at Stanford. I didn't mind "crippled," but I did really object to the "little." It took some time to acclimate to a different way of thinking about identity. At the UN, for example, I learned that one cannot put two women from different African nations in the same office space unless there existed cultural cooperation between the two countries. Or, despite the collapse of the Soviet Union, a person could still deeply identify with that culture. "I'm a Soviet woman," a woman from the former USSR insisted. "So please don't call me a Russian because that is not who I am." At the UN, nationality and cultural identity were the first words of introduction and conversation after meeting someone the first time.

It was around this time, and in this mindset, when I began down the path of thinking about diversity, equity, and inclusion as part of my leadership journey. But it would still be a few more years before I had really clarified my own ideas, acknowledged my personal journey, and built a strategy for "others" to matter and belong.

Hitting That Famous Glass Ceiling

My parents' fears about Y2K caused my return to the United States. I moved back to California and landed a job at a national firm that was headquartered in Wisconsin. It was so close to home, in fact, that the CEO was a patient of my father. At my first partner dinner, the CEO sat down next to me and proclaimed, in front of all my new partners, that he had just seen my father and was happy to announce that his colonoscopy was clean and he had no polyps! (Luckily, with a gastroenterologist for a father, I had discussed plenty worse at the dinner table, so this hardly fazed me at all!) Nevertheless, I always wondered if, in that moment, it looked like I had landed the job through nepotism, rather than hard work.

For the next decade, I worked on my craft as a trial attorney and a leader of teams. I led the Northern California offices of the firm, addressed and remedied financial issues, opened and closed offices, and focused on equity and inclusion in the West Coast region. Because I had early success in California, the CEO asked me to be the LGBT partner on the newly formed diversity committee. This meant I had to be openly gay to over four hundred people, most of whom I had never met. Over a short period of time, I felt my career go sideways. On the surface, the CEO wanted the firm to lead other law firms in diversity programs and metrics. We had a brochure high-lighting the diversity within the company. Behind closed doors, things were more complicated. I learned firsthand from this experience that it doesn't matter if a few people at the top have the best of intentions regarding diversity metrics if the rest of the organization is not aligned with the values of equity and inclusion. On the surface, it seemed like the whole firm was supportive of the initiative. At best, it was just a superficial makeover—something that looks good to clients and has no real staying power. These check-the-box initiatives result in harm to the individuals who stand up for a culture shift that is not supported by systemic change.

> **It doesn't matter if a few people at the top have the best of intentions ... if the rest of the organization is not aligned with the values of equity and inclusion.**

Learning to Start Again

As a leader at the law firm, I applied the process I learned from MKM to evaluate what worked and what didn't. I didn't want to be the leader that just checked the box with good PR without making any real strides down the path of equity and inclusion. I wanted a truly holistic process for transforming a company, both from the top down and the ground up, into a truly equitable and inclusive place to work.

In this time of self-reflection, I left the practice of law. I hit a professional and personal roadblock. How could I ask people to see and accept one another, to see the value in each other's differences, if I had never really come to accept and value myself? In this way, the process of doing this work at a professional level has also been the very personal work of coming to accept my own identity. There is a Rumi quote that I have come to be fond of: "Yesterday I was clever, so I wanted to change the world. Today I am wise, so I am changing myself." I love this quote because it speaks to my own experience. My contribution to this bit of wisdom is to encourage people to get to that "today" moment as early as possible. As we get better at seeing and accepting ourselves, it gets easier to be curious and see others as well.

Fred Rogers, the famous children's television host of *Mister Rogers' Neighborhood*, once said, "Anything that's human is mentionable, and anything that is mentionable can be more manageable. When we can talk about our feelings, they become less overwhelming, less upsetting, and less scary. The people we trust with that important talk can help us know that we are not alone." I share a shortened version of this quote in my workshops: "What is mentionable is manageable." No problem has ever been solved by pretending it doesn't exist or hoping the problem will go away. James Baldwin states, "Not everything that is faced can be changed, but nothing can be changed until it is faced."

The unfortunate events that inspired movements like #MeToo and Black Lives Matter have shined a light on and given voice to the importance of equity and inclusion in the workplace. We can have conversations about identity, bias, and microaggressions in a way that we never have before. We are learning about our own triggers and defensive behaviors. We understand that biases exist, and by naming them, we can make the unconscious conscious. By mentioning these biases and microaggressions, we can manage our behaviors.

An Invitation to All

In my own life, the framing of my journey toward self-acceptance had a lot to do with my sexuality, and later, with my disabilities. But for someone else, this experience might look extremely different, especially if they aren't used to thinking in terms of "identity." Often it is straight, white, able-bodied cisgender men who have a hard time seeing themselves through the lens of identity.[8] We all have histories, and we are more than our identities. Our current culture doesn't always prepare us to see everyone's identities as clearly as our own. We are not just one identity; nor does one's identity represent all.

In a recent diversity training, I met a senior leader, whom we'll call Joe, who self-identified as a white, Episcopalian, middle-aged man. Joe confided in me that he thought this DEI stuff was "just bonk." It was his opinion that one should "just work hard, do your job; that's all." I thought for a bit about how to respond to Joe and then asked him to tell me his story. "Tell me about your high school

---

8   "Cisgender," or "cis," means that the gender you identify with matches the sex assigned to you at birth. This differs from transgender, where your gender identity is not the sex on your birth certificate.

experience. Which group were you in? Were you a nerd? A theater kid? A jock?"

Joe looked at me and then responded, "Well, I wasn't any of those things. I was really the class clown."

"So, were you happy being the class clown?" I asked.

"Well, I loved getting laughs."

"Do you still do that today?"

"Well, yes, I suppose."

"Why do you think you do this?"

He thought about this for a bit and then answered, "I guess it's the way I know that I fit in, that people like me."

"Bingo! That's it. That's an example of your story, of trying to matter and to belong." As I said this, I saw something click for Joe. Even though he didn't think of his own identities—he didn't want to acknowledge identity generally—he had attached his sense of self, of belonging, to making people laugh. It was an integral part of his identity. Deep down, everybody, even Joe, wants to be accepted and fit in. We work hard to develop these skills and identities to be seen and heard. When you reframe equity and inclusion as another way of saying mattering and belonging, suddenly it becomes something that everyone wants and needs, regardless of the labels we use to see differences.

When we don't feel like we belong, we don't feel safe. The desire for safety is a powerful motivator. We seek it out in our families, in our workplaces, and in our wider communities. We are not our best selves when we don't feel safe. That little animal brain, the amygdala and the limbic system, gets triggered. Fear controls. It overrides our ability to think until we clear the emotions that fear provokes. We often talk about "fight or flight" when we talk about fear responses, but there is a third option, and that's to hide. Joe hid his feelings about belonging and became the "class clown." He entertained as a means of belonging. People liked him, and he liked being liked. When we fear being rejected, we hide our otherness. This was the way that I learned to protect myself in the workplace. And while I was able to advance in my professional life, up to a point, I never really felt I was doing my best work until I was able to stop hiding and to start encouraging others to do the same.

Several months later, Joe returned to another diversity training. "I wrote down my story, like you encouraged me to," he told me. "I learned a lot. I even shared it with some friends and family members. I was the super smart guy, the nerd, who didn't want to be teased or left out." Joe did the work himself by writing his own history. For the first time, Joe saw how vulnerability and empathy develops trust, which could, in time, help rather than hinder his relationships with his team and his clients.

It had never occurred to him that other people in the workplace had to hide their identities to feel like part of the gang. Once he saw that, Joe didn't want to be the reason others had to hide. He began to encourage his coworkers to write their stories and even to share them as well. He realized that the work of a high-performing team is the work of equity and inclusion. Joe focused on creating psychological safety for his colleagues to be their full and best selves at work. The process of opening to see people wholly, whether spoken or unspoken, creates a productive and dynamic team, which inevitably builds an engaging workplace for all.

Lead by Example

Everyone has the power to move forward and share their story. The skill sets required to create psychological safety are learned through preparation and practice. As a leader in the workplace, Joe's ability to admit when he didn't know something, and to be open to learning, was a signal to his colleagues that they didn't have to have all the answers either. Joe showed a commitment to figuring things out together and to prioritizing the work of belonging and mattering. It's this work, based on creating an environment that feels psychologically safe, that we are now calling equity and inclusion. Even if you, like Joe, have wondered what is "the point" of this focus on self, story, and identity, I invite you to open yourself to this work and to the possibility of the changes (both in yourself and in your professional life) that it can offer.

The Takeaways

If you walk away from this chapter with just a few main ideas, here are some good ones:

1. Approach everything with a childlike curiosity. Stay curious longer.

2. Enjoy being a beginner and the journey toward mastery, which never ends.

3. Figure out what your unique ability is—what comes easily and effortlessly to you? What do you love doing?

4. Get comfortable in your own skin, and the sooner you can do this, the better.

5. Everyone has a very deep need to be seen and heard, to achieve and be accepted, to belong and to matter.

CHAPTER 2

Your People

A boss tells people what they must do to achieve a goal. A leader asks people what they can do to advance a vision.

—SIMON SINEK, *START WITH WHY*

Leadership is, above all, about giving of yourself. Your time and your attention are the most valuable resources that you can give to your team. It's your job to make sure that your stakeholders—your customers, your team, and your suppliers, even your wider network—feel seen and heard. They need to know that they matter, that they belong, and that they are vital, even in some small way, to the wider vision you are working together to create.

This chapter is intended to give you the tools you need to lead better, to focus on the people around you, and to recognize that leadership is about *being* rather than *doing*. It's about painting a compelling vision, creating openings and opportunities, and providing the resources and tools needed by your team to join you on your journey toward that shared vision. It's about creating space for others to speak and to listen with curiosity.

Recognize That You Are a Team

Often people who want to become leaders start with a focus on themselves in the workplace: "What do I do?" "What do I say?" "How should I act?" As new leaders, we cloak ourselves in anticipation of how we are "supposed" to be. Self-awareness and empathy are personal work that leaders must do. While it's important to do the personal work on leadership, the simplest thing you can do as a leader is refocus your attention on your team—the people you work with—instead of yourself. These same questions must be asked of your team. "What do you do at work?" "What do you love about your work?" What's working for you?" "What's not working?" "What tools or resources are needed to do more of what's working?" Rather than only telling my stories of learning and leadership, I ask questions that invite others to tell their stories. I am curious about the lived experiences of others.

It's also common for people new to leadership to think that being a leader means having all the answers. I often hear the statement that "a leader is the person who knows what to do and dictates the manner in which the team should complete the project." Leadership is not about the title or about knowing the answers. It is a function that engages, inspires, and motivates the team toward an explicit goal. Exceptional leaders focus on developing the skill sets of the team and setting the tone for the cross-functional work that is required from all. As we move into this next era of business leadership—what people are calling "twenty-first-century leadership"—the reality is we are leaning into the idea that empathy, sympathy, and being open and vulnerable are vital to the notion of successful leadership.

More and more, new research[9] is showing us that the best leaders, the ones who lead the best teams that run the best companies, aren't the ones who have all the answers. The most effective leaders are actually the ones who figure out the right questions to ask, the right person or people to ask it to, and how to ask the question in such a way that the geniuses in the room—that's the team—are able to speak up and act with integrity and accountability. These teams are thriving, uniquely as individuals and collectively as a high-performance team.

That's why it's so important to have the right people in your sphere of influence. Without a doubt, your team is your competitive advantage. I've heard leaders say "I want smart people around me. I want to be the dumbest person in the room." While I understand this sentiment, I want to caution against too much prioritizing of intelligence or pedigree. You can have a whole boardroom of people who went to Stanford, Harvard, and Yale, but if they all come from similar backgrounds and share a common perspective, that's not a winning team for the long game. Because research[10] also indicates that the teams that are the most successful at strategy, risk management, and innovation are those that come from a diversity of lived experiences, voice a diversity of thought, and are comfortable with vigorous debate. As a leader, you aren't just looking for that one best idea; you are really looking for all the ideas on which the team

> **As a leader, you aren't just looking for that one best idea; you are really looking for all the ideas on which the team will build.**

---

9   Brené Brown, featuring Adam Grant and Simon Sinek, "What's Happening at Work: Part 1" *Dare to Lead* podcast, October 03, 2022, 40:42; Part 2, October 10, 2020, 42:05.

10 Hewlett, Marshall, and Sherbin, "How Diversity Can Drive Innovation."

will build. A team built on diverse identities, on a multiplicity of lived experiences, will give you a variety of ideas and perspectives that a team made of people with the same outlook as one another would never be able to provide.

"Bend the Universe"

Having the vision and the right team isn't enough. Your team must also learn to *trust* both in one another and in the greater vision of the company. They are smart and attentive people. Know that they see you and expect you to model the values and vision as well. Do your actions match your words? Do your core values match that vision? Because that's what lifts the organization well above the competition and creates not only a high-performing team but also a fun team, a team that is ready and willing to "bend the universe" with you. Bending the universe is really about culture shift. It's evolutionary and revolutionary; a process that every growing business must embrace to scale.

You may have heard the phrase "We're here to make a dent in the universe," which is often attributed to Steve Jobs. Well, I would like to offer a slight revision to this sentiment. The problem, as I see it, with the word "dent" is all about fighting, demolition, and destruction. These metaphors come from a feeling of scarcity rather than a place of abundance. But the universe isn't a cherry pie, and there really is enough to go around. That's why I like to say "bend the universe," because bending is a softer, gentler maneuver, arching in the direction we'd like things to go rather than from a place of force. Once there is a dent or a crack, the tool is unreliable. Bending the universe focuses on flexibility and adaptability.

Think Like a Coach

Transitioning from being a player to being the coach, or from being a team member to being the leader, is a complex and challenging shift. As business leaders, we are used to achieving and doing it all on our own. We are the center of attention, the hero who scores the winning goal. Often, when former players take on the role of coach, they struggle to let go of being the skilled player—one who "does"—and have difficulty embracing the importance of all players on the team. A good leader views the whole field and each player as an integral part of the team. The lens is wider and longer. A good leader, like a good coach, lets go of that self-dependence and need for glory. Ultimately, good leaders, working on mastery, know that they are here to do something different.

A coach doesn't do everything themselves—they can't. Instead, a coach is really a leader and a manager. Management is about keeping your expectations clear, communicating well and often, and rewarding and recognizing the efforts of your team. It's about taking all the disparate skill sets that live inside of people and bringing them together. Good coaches bring out the best in everyone so the disparate parts achieve greater goals, making the impossible seem possible. Management is about trust. A talented team will win some games based on talent and lose some games to a better team. I often ask whether the winning goal is the first one or the last. If there is a high level of trust in the coach and among team members, the team will perform at a higher level and continue to improve beyond the individual skill sets. This is the human example that a trusting team is better than the sum of its parts. Sometimes players may not understand in the moment why they are doing what they are doing. A good leader explains the value of the contribution. If that team member trusts the leader, on and off the "court," extraordinary achievements happen. It doesn't mean that team always wins. It doesn't mean that the team will achieve every specific goal. In sports, we often reward success that happens only 30 percent of the time. Better than 70 percent is doing better than most competitors. A trusting team is learning and moving toward a culture of innovation and excellence. The leader's purpose, much like a coach, is to bring out the best in people by rewarding effort, innovation, and execution.

Set the Stage: My Meeting Practice

The first step to build safety among team members is to make sure that everything from the physical working environment to the workplace energy feels inviting and comfortable. Some people refer to this as "holding the space." But it's not enough to just say "We're going to hold the space." It takes time, it takes practice, and sometimes it's full of contradictions. Holding the space means creating an environment where people are curious. The team learns to feel comfortable sharing, speaking their mind to voice an opinion, and holding one another accountable (rather than speaking out to other people once they leave the room). Stated another way, the team is calling each other "in" rather than calling each other "out." These high-performing teams have a zero tolerance for gossip and a "no shame and no blame" approach to accountability.

In preparation for any meeting, whether in person, online, or hybrid, it's important that I set the "stage" prior to the meeting's start. This also has the effect of settling my own energy, shifting my focus, and preparing my mindset for what's ahead. I arrive early and take stock of the room. I'll sit in many different chairs in the room so that my presence is additive and not a hindrance to the purpose of the meeting. I consider the physical characteristics of the room. Is this a hybrid meeting? Will the table mikes, camera, and monitor be visible to all? Who needs to use the whiteboard? Are the markers reliable? What is the lighting like? Is the temperature comfortable? As the younger people on my team would say, I like to "feel the vibe" of the space.

If the meeting includes remote team members, I turn on the camera and observe the lighting, what I look like, and what's in the background before anyone else joins the meeting. Is there anything strange or distracting in the background that I should move off screen? I don't want the environment to be distracting, triggering, or isolating.

I'll often ask a few pertinent questions to myself out loud. "Why am I here? What am I here to do?" Asking myself these questions helps me remember that I matter and belong so I can get my ego out of the way and be present for the participants. I find it's helpful to hear my voice in the space and, at the same time, to remind myself of the vision and the purpose that drives me. I do some breathing exercises and get ready to go! While teaching and coaching come naturally to me, I use up a lot of energy in the moment. I have learned over time how to channel my energies and to create a warm and welcoming space for others to enter. It requires ongoing work, focus, and energy.

Practicing "people skills" also means holding the space through the whole meeting, not just at the beginning. I visualize the entire agenda, step by step, in my head. I like to write out the objectives of the meeting on the board. I go through and identify the items on the agenda that are likely to generate strong emotions, both positive and negative, and prepare myself to listen with curiosity. This helps me anticipate my own triggers and take a needed pause before I respond. I have learned that pausing gives me the opportunity to evaluate whether my response is meaningful and relevant to the topic at hand. I am prepared for the unexpected.

I am always overly prepared, knowing that nothing ever goes as planned. I prepare for the technical glitches. I prepare for meeting distractions such as people joining late or walking in while on the phone. I make a point of thanking those who are ready to start on time. I start on time, stick to the agenda, and finish on time, out of respect for the team's time. When necessary, I have a one-on-one conversation with a team member who does not respect the team's time.

Check In

Everyone on my team learns quickly that my meetings always start on time. They arrive early and take the time to settle into the meeting. While it's unavoidable that someone is going to come in late on occasion, they know to enter, sit down, and not distract the meeting in process. If they feel the need to explain themselves, the next break is a proper time to do this, not during the meeting. At first, this might take some getting accustomed to, and people will exclaim, "You started without me." It only takes a couple of these occurrences before something clicks, and a person's punctuality and accountability level bump up a notch.

Once everyone has arrived and settled into the room, beginning with a short group activity has the effect of creating a space to transition into the meeting agenda and objectives. Collectively, the team readies itself to work. Each member of the team transitions from the prior activity—getting the kids to school on time, rushing to the meeting, finishing a call, getting coffee, or having a critical conversation with a colleague. We use this time to arrive and remember who we are to each other and what we represent to our team.

One activity our team likes is "Personal and Professional Best." In this exercise, each member of the team takes one quiet minute to write down their personal and professional best moment since the last time we met. Just a sentence or so each is enough. Then we go around the room and share what we wrote down with one another. Another transition activity is to simply sit in silence for sixty seconds. Each team member uses the time to "Be Here, Now." If the energy in the room seems off or unexpectedly emotional, we use the time after the silence to regain focus. As a leader, I facilitate the energy in the room. Personal, business, or current events might take precedence over a planned agenda. Leaders adapt and take care of the team. There really is nothing to say that can alleviate personal pain, and yet we can't ignore it's presence. Sometimes, it's enough to simply breathe together and hold the space, in the acknowledgment that the world, with all its pain, pressing issues, and complexities, still spins all around us. You can't build a high-performance team if you pretend otherwise or if you refuse to acknowledge the big events in the world, our communities, our families, and our lives.

The teams that I have worked with for years understand that this transition time is part of what makes this space feel safe. I also have found that this creates what I like to call "structured serendipity." I've had meetings that have taken a left turn when I thought we were turning right because we took this time to ground ourselves. Adaptability in this regard builds trust. The team feels the empathy and caring of the leader who sees each member of the team uniquely. A leader may walk in thinking that the team is going to talk about X, but because of something that is happening in real time, the team takes time to get everyone seen and heard. The key to adaptability is about being present, being comfortable, and being prepared. In this way, the leader can adjust if necessary and bring the team back to the original agenda without causing harm.

A strong, creative leader is managing human energy, physical and emotional. Most of our decisions are based on our emotions, and we use logic to justify the choice. Acknowledging that your team is human, that emotions exist, that every member needs to matter and belong, your team will show up in extraordinary ways and achieve extraordinary results.

Lean into Diversity

After nearly sixty years, beginning with the entry of women into the workplace and incorporating and acknowledging BIPOC (Black, Indigenous, and People of Color) and LGBTQ+ colleagues, the evidence is irrefutable,[11] whether it comes from McKinsey, Pew, Bain, or Stanford. The more diverse a team is, the more they bring a multiplicity of experiences and identities, the better their performance when measured against the competition.

The work of having a diverse team starts with expanding the pool of applicants and the places where the company sources these applicants. Many publicly traded corporations claim that they are extraordinarily diverse; however, if that diversity is simply at the warehouse level, not at the level of leadership, it won't produce sustainable change in the company. From the mail room to the boardroom, the true competitive advantage happens only when that diversity is reflected in all teams, from bottom to top, at all levels of the organization.

---

11   Hunt, Prince, Dolan, and Dixon-Fyle, "Diversity Wins"; "Getting to Equal: The Disability Inclusion Advantage," Accenture, 2018, https://www.accenture.com/_acnmedia/pdf-89/accenture-disability-inclusion-research-report.pdf; Hunt, Layon, and Prince, "Diversity Matters"; Pew, The Great Resignation, 2022.

If you don't work to increase the equity and inclusion aspects of your organization's culture, the company will lose those A players. Equity is about creating a company that creates opportunities and provides tools and resources for each person individually, so that every person can thrive. Inclusion is the creation of the mindset and mentality in your team that each person, each individual, has a voice that is valued and respected. It's about mattering. Hiring for diversity is about looking for candidates in new, often unfamiliar places, focusing on skill sets and not résumé highlights.

Diversity isn't just one label, one skill set, or a one-dimensional identity. We are made up of a kaleidoscope of identities and lived experiences. Each person is their own blend of "The Big Eight" socially constructed identities: race, ethnicity, sexual orientation, gender identity, ability, religion/spirituality, nationality, and socio-economic status. Additionally, while a kaleidoscope of identities and lived experiences around the conference table is important, a good leader welcomes different learning styles and different communication styles to create a high-performance team.

It's important to understand that just as no one is a singular identity, no one person can represent an entire group of people. A team member who is African American does not represent every African American in the United States, nor should they have to speak about that experience in general terms. Too often, BIPOC and LGBTQ+ people are asked to bear the burden of educating their white and straight colleagues about what it feels like to be BIPOC or LGBTQ+. One member of a marginalized group is not and should not be the spokesperson for all who share the same skin color or sexual identity. Within every marginalized community, there are a multitude of lived experiences, because no one of us is just a single identity.

Just as it can be hurtful to overly emphasize one aspect of a person's identity, it can also be hurtful to negate or ignore these things as well. Occasionally, I hear people say "Well, I don't see color" or "I treat everyone the same, regardless of where they're from." Even though they may be striving for equality, refusing to acknowledge a person's race negates their lived experience. "We're all in the same storm; we're just not in the same boat." We have many experiences in common, and we aren't all the same. A Jewish person may need to take a personal day for Yom Kippur and will work the days before and after Christmas. A person of Muslim faith may need a place and time to pray during the workday. The majority has a sanctioned holiday for Christmastime. As leaders, we need to examine systemic policies that celebrate our different lived experiences rather than perpetuate inequitable treatment.

All too often, I hear people responding with defensiveness when they are asked to see and acknowledge their colleagues' kaleidoscope of identities. Out of a sense of discomfort, they will move the conversation away from their colleague or refocus it on themselves. They might say "Oh, I also have a disability too," when asked to see and acknowledge their colleague's needs for additional productivity tools. Or "I get it; my sister is gay," when asked to include a gay colleague's spouse at the company picnic. Even if the intention may have been to empathize with their teammate, this kind of self-centering language inevitably shuts down the conversation. The shift in focus denigrates the vulnerability and emotional risk of the disclosure to a colleague. Over time, the wall of defensiveness negatively affects performance and erodes trust.

When one is made aware of the harm caused by self-centering, it's not difficult to repair. A correction such as "I'm sorry; I didn't mean to dismiss your experience as a gay person. I need to know about you.

Would you consider a do-over?" Every person wants to be seen for who they are. The opportunity or invitation is the pivotal moment of equity and inclusion. Impact is the key, not the intent of the speaker. Acknowledgments and apologies are just a first step in the equity and inclusion journey. Apologies must be genuine and sincere with a promise to improve and an invitation to be called out in the moment, regardless of the context.

Build a Team of Others

Plenty of articles in business magazines like *Entrepreneur* or *Inc.* will tell you that being a better leader for your team is all about the doing. "Do these five activities every day to be an empathetic leader." Rarely do you read the simplest advice: ask a question; be curious. If you want to be a better leader, if you want to create more psychological safety for your teammates, just ask: "What do you need to be your best today? How can I show up better for you?" The more you learn about the people on your team, the more you will begin to see the multiplicity of experiences and identities that they hold dear. These lived experiences and kaleidoscope of identities are the superpowers of a Team of Others. We become better team members when we know and trust our teammates.

I spend a lot of time listening and observing with intention and attention. I listen to the space between the words and watch how the speaker's body communicates. I gauge the temperature of the individuals and the group, their responses to various events, information, and conflict. I particularly pay attention to the gaps of silence. Because it's the thoughts that aren't expressed verbally that get in the way of building trust with a team. Without that trust, growth is slow and full of suffering. I use the mantra "If you think it, say it" to build effective teams. The bravest person on the team may make a brief foray with a direct statement. Sometimes its awkward and full of caveats. As a team, we are patient and pay close attention to the "real" message.

Whether it's a one-on-one conversation about the allocation of resources or a leadership team of fifty working on a strategic plan, it's important to acknowledge that people crave the leader's time and attention. Being an active listener, asking questions, showing interest in the response, observing, and acknowledging the power of the group signifies to the team that they are seen and heard. Feeling and knowing that your voice matters is what creates the psychological safety necessary for a high-performing team. Encouragement of conflict, better known to some as vigorous debate, helps teams learn to tolerate differing or dissenting opinions. When facilitating a challenging and important conversation, I desensitize the discussion by asking "What does the company need from us as a leadership team?"

Our brains process information primarily through nonverbal cues. According to studies by behavioral psychologist Dr. Albert Mehrabian,[12] 55 percent of our communication pertaining to feelings and attitudes is expressed through facial expression, 38 percent is through the tone and cadence of our voices, and only 7 percent is actually the words that are spoken. This has come to be known as the 7-38-55 rule.[13] Learning to pay attention to these cues, consciously, gives the leader the most information about the feelings and emotions of the individuals on the team. A good leader knows to inquire what it means when someone tilts their head or crosses their arms. Someone

---

12   "Mehrabian's 7-38-55 Communication Model: It's More Than Words," World of Work Project, accessed December 2022, https://worldofwork.io/2019/07/mehrabians-7-38-55-communication-model/.

13   Jon Michail, "Strong Nonverbal Skills Matter Now More Than Ever In This 'New Normal'" *Forbes*, August 24, 2020, https://www.forbes.com/sites/forbescoaches-council/2020/08/24/strong-nonverbal-skills-matter-now-more-than-ever-in-this-new-normal/?sh=4842a35d5c61.

could be agreeing with their words but disagreeing with their body language. They could have a great idea flashing through their mind that just needs a little goading to come out. It's important not to miss these moments of expression, because they indicate the feelings and emotions in the room. These nonverbal cues build or contribute to the ideas that precede innovation and transformation. A leader who stays curious and vulnerable is listening for the build of the ideas that drive toward a decision that is in the best interests of the company.

Listening with intention means that you are striving to see the story in the speaker's mind, and not creating your own narrative. This is an incredibly important distinction because our minds are so used to creating our own movies in our heads. The work of connection is to get outside of yourself. Imagining the other person's story helps us see and understand their struggles and achievements. Your mind becomes more wired toward empathy. Just the words "I get you" or "I understand" have such a deep power for making connections and getting personal.

> **Building a company, a team, and a culture that creates the experience of safety in its members isn't a simple thing.**

Build Trust

While it's easy to say you want to build a team that trusts one another, it's much harder to achieve this. Trust is psychological safety to think it and say it. That's where great effort and achievement happens. Building a company, a team, and a culture that creates the experience of safety in its members isn't a simple thing. It's an orientation, a process that requires persistent intention and constant attention. Luckily, there are many well-documented story-telling exercises you can do to build trust and a feeling of community and commonality among your team.

Business management expert Patrick Lencioni recommends doing what he calls the "Personal Histories" exercise. In this exercise, each member of the team writes down their answers to five questions about their personal lives. Some examples include the following: Where did you grow up? What was your best job? What was your worst job? What did you like about college? What did you hate about college?[14] Once everyone has completed their answers to the questions, each person takes five minutes to share their answers. As a listener, it's not your job to ask questions or offer advice or recommendations. As a listener, you are responsible only for keeping an open mind, and listening with focus and attention, to learn something new about your teammates. Other exercises Lencioni suggests are playing "Never have I ever" and "Two truths and a lie." While these exercises may seem like silly games played in summer camp or college, they invite people to let down their guard and to speak freely and openly. This vulnerability is the key to having people understand why they're there, to see how they connect with one another, and to build the shared vision of high performance and success.

Understanding the Critter Brain

Taking the time to have your team members connect with one another on a very human, very personal level is an excellent step toward seeing one another as individuals full of multiple, complex identities. We have ancient brains. The middle part of our brain controls our emotions and short-term memory, while the oldest part of our

---

14   Patrick Lencioni, *The Five Dysfunctions of a Team* (San Francisco: Jossey-Bass, 2002).

brain, our limbic system, a.k.a. the "critter" brain, is responsible for the behaviors we need for survival: feeding, reproduction, caring for our young, and of course, the famous fight or flight. These primal instincts are hardwired; we are instinctually and constantly scanning for threats and interpreting danger. As much as we think of ourselves as rational, logical, evolved creatures, the truth is about 90 percent of our decision-making happens in these ancient parts of our mind.[15] Then, the more evolved part, the neocortex, or frontal lobe, interprets these emotions. It rationalizes the decisions made by the critter brain, making plans and strategizing to affirm the decision. Many of our teammates still experience physical danger every day on the drive to work or out for a run. Those of us with privilege are rarely in physical danger.

In the business world, danger shows up as a threat to the status quo. Our critter brains are still hard wired to fight or flight, and in a conference room, fight looks like anger and flight looks like a physical or a psychological exit. A physical exit is easy to identify; it's someone walking out of the room in a huff. But a psychological exit is harder to spot. The teammate that leans back in their chair, arms folded, face turned down or away has clearly checked out mentally. While this might seem like the behavior of a sullen teenager, the reality is that this behavior is unconscious and automatic as a defensive response to a perceived threat. The most difficult is the A player who is just silent, withholding ideas and opportunities because she is not seen and thus not heard. After a time, psychological exits result in resignations, which create instability and significant costs for the organization.

---

15   J. S. Lerner and D. Kletner, "Beyond Valence," *Cognition and Emotion* 14 (2000); J. S. Lerner, D. A. Smaill, and G. Lowenstein, "Heart Strings and Purse Strings," *Psychological Science* 15 (2004); G. Zaltman, *How Customers Think* (Boston: Harvard Business School Press, 2003).

In these moments, we must recognize our own trigger patterns that signify fear or threat. I recognize that I am in a critter state when my hands get moist. I pick at my cuticles. My breathing becomes shallow and faster. My neck colors red. I know that, for myself, my defensive reaction to fear is often anger. I react with anger when I get surprised or my status quo is threatened. I have learned how to identify and interrupt that pattern because I have invited my team to hold me accountable by asking an open-ended and pointed question about my discomfort with the topic or the issue. I pause and acknowledge that I am not in mortal danger. I identify the emotion and interrupt it; I calm myself by figuratively and literally getting oxygen to my brain with a breathing exercise. At that moment of calm, I clearly see the information that is coming my way. If I am emotional, then I'm not thinking, and I can't process information. What I want to do is to interrupt that unconscious thought process before it becomes words or actions that cause harm to others.

Understand Your Biases

Unconscious thought patterns show up all the time in our interactions with one another. We get triggered by a colleague's frown, the turn of a head, the crossing of the arms, or a simple statement that indicates conflict.

Recently I was working with a team in which one team member felt that another member didn't like her and didn't appreciate her contributions. She didn't understand the why. She was upset that she was never invited out after work with her colleagues, and it caused her to doubt herself and lose self-esteem. At a team meeting I facilitated the conflict between the two. We dug deep into why her teammate didn't like her and discovered that she reminded her teammate of his hypercritical soccer coach from when he was ten years old. He realized that he was unconsciously projecting this association of his childhood nemesis onto this woman. When he shared the association, they began to realize that, despite it all, they had a lot in common. He loved soccer, his kids played soccer, and she had also played soccer in college, so they were able to form a connection around the very thing that had caused friction in the past. Reliving the emotional trigger and telling the story out loud to the team made the issue manageable. What is mentionable is manageable.

Race triggers unconscious biases, especially when we don't have much exposure to people of other races. I work with a team that recently gained a new member who was a tall, fit Black man. Peter, one of the white men on the team, was excited for him to join, because Peter was sure the new team member must play and enjoy basketball. Rashad, the new team member, was nothing like what Peter had anticipated. During his self-introduction to the team, Rashad announced that he loved theater and was willing to work Christian holidays because he was Muslim. To connect with Rashad, Peter tried to engage Rashad about basketball. In addition to his disappointment that Rashad was not athletic, Peter's unconscious bias that "Muslims are dangerous" resulted in passive-aggressive conflict between the two. During a facilitated quarterly meeting on goals and team building, a third team member raised the issue of Peter's passive-aggressive behavior toward Rashad. After significant coaching and personal work, Peter acknowledged that he was embarrassed by his behavior caused by his stereotyped assumptions. Rather than be curious about Rashad, Peter hid his shame and ignorance behind his behavior. Fortunately for Peter and Rashad, the team had done significant trust-building work such that a third team member felt compelled to raise the issue.

Bias exists in all of us. Working on self-awareness helps to identify the situations in which we feel threatened. Bias and the unconscious behaviors that result from bias negatively affect psychological safety in the workplace. "I get scary when I am threatened." A Black coworker is told he can't play music in the office because a coworker connects two beliefs. "Black people only listen to rap music, and rap music is dangerous." A team member who has dyslexia is given more time to complete her tasks because her manager has lower expectations about her abilities. Over time, she began to feel that she wasn't really being held to the same standards as her nondyslexic peers, and her performance began to decrease. However, it wasn't her dyslexia that caused her work ethic to slump but the lowered expectations around her abilities. These beliefs, acted on by managers, are microaggressions that cause harm to the person, which ultimately affects performance.

Interrupt Unconscious Actions

Logic makes people think, whereas emotions make people act. The goal is to take the unconscious and make it conscious. Challenge yourself and your teammates to ask these questions: Am I safe? What assumptions am I making about this person? Do I have resources that help my productivity? Is this a place of abundance rather than scarcity? Learn to apply that childlike curiosity to learn about others and listen with patience and creativity.

Microaggressions are often quick and unintentional. They are woven into the fabric of the everyday language that we use. To say that you have "blind spots" implies that there is something negative about having low vision. To say you want to "keep the trains running on time" is a phrase that is emblematic of the discipline the Nazis used to ship Jews to the concentration camps. Without meaning to cause harm, these phrases can negate and nullify the thoughts, feelings, and experiences of the person right across the table from you. They accumulate over time, so that by the time you see that person storm out of the room, they have been absorbing microaggressions (whether they know it or not) for some time. The harm is cumulative.

It's the responsibility of the leader to shift the culture and interrupt these patterns of attack and defensiveness. Many of the phrases we use every day to illustrate a point have a "difficult" origin. Be open to correction. Breathe deeply. If the words or actions are harmful, listen intently when the concern is raised. Breathe deeply, again. Again, be open to correction. Apologize instead of defending your words or actions. Understand that impact is more important than intent. Ask how to resolve the tension or conflict. Ask for a do-over, and do better. Complete the practice with an affirmation of appreciation. These small harms add up over time. They negatively affect performance and contribute to a feeling of not belonging and not mattering.

Because so many of these instances are unintentional, it really doesn't take much effort to shift a person's behavior. A team that cares about the well-being of one another shares the accountability for building trust. Using game theory to identify bias and microaggressions does a great deal to lessen the impact of the criticism. I have used sports language such as "Yellow flag, penalty on the play" or "Foul ball, you're still at bat" as I am pointing out the misstep. This does wonders for lessening a person's automatic defense mechanisms. The team quickly gets to the place of acknowledgment, apology, and a do-over that expresses their message without the harmful language.

Get Comfortable Being Uncomfortable

Darwin was famous for explaining that evolution was the process of the "survival of the fittest." Most people think "fittest" meant the fastest, the strongest, and the smartest creatures. According to Darwin, the fittest creatures are the most adaptable. Humans have a much greater likelihood of thriving when we lean into adaptability—to really look at ourselves, to recognize our biases and gaps in understanding, and to be willing to grow and change.

If you want to be a leader, you must be willing to get out of your comfort zone. Yes, it's going to be awkward, and you are going to make mistakes, but you can also use these mistakes as opportunities to show your team that it's okay to make mistakes. A simple "Ah, darn it, I blew it," without getting defensive or shutting down, will do wonders for leading by example on how to handle critiques.

"You know who the happiest animal in the world is? A goldfish. Why? It's got a ten-second memory."[16] I think there is something to having a short memory. (And if you haven't seen the *Ted Lasso* show, I recommend it. It's got some great stuff about leadership.) The piece of advice that Coach Lasso omits is the commitment to improve. The reality is, when we talk about leadership and goals, what we are talking about is looking forward, not backward. We are talking about making those constant adjustments in the moment. So be a goldfish, and when you mess up, be willing to acknowledge it publicly with an apology and a commitment to do better.

When your teammates see that you can handle the tension of disagreement or of being wrong, it helps to build trust. When you go through an uncomfortable event as a team, it helps to build, not

---

16   Ted Lasso, "Biscuits," season 1, episode 2, writer Joe Kelly, dir. Zach Braff, AppleTV+, August 14, 2020.

harm, the psychological safety of the group. The entire team learns that they can trust one another, that they can ride the waves of conflict and disagreement together, and will get through to the other side stronger than before.

The Takeaways

1. Be a coach of the different skill sets and lived experiences of your team.

2. Show your team your intention with attention.

3. Build a Team of Others that acts for the good of the company.

4. Recognize your biases and set the intention of interrupting them, making the unconscious conscious.

5. Recognize that discomfort isn't a bad thing; it's an indicator of growth. Apologize and do better. There is no try.

CHAPTER 3

Your Presence

---

*You are what you think. Think it today; become
it tomorrow. Nothing can help you or hurt you as
much as the thoughts you carry in your head.*

—ZEN BUDDHIST QUOTE

About twenty-five years ago, I attended a workshop in which the
participants were invited to take a very long, very involved multiple-
choice "test" to assess our strengths and weaknesses as leaders. In that
ego-centric frame of mind, I was sure that I could skew my answers to
the result I preferred. This assessment however was so extensive that
there was no way to "game" it. I took the test openly and honestly,
secure in my abilities to test as a better-than-average leader.

When we got the results back, I was shocked. While I displayed
strengths in almost all aspects of leadership, there was one area where I
showed a glaring deficiency: empathy. As a default emotion, I tested in
the bottom tenth percentile of the thousands of leaders who had taken
the assessment. I considered myself an empathetic person. When I

shared this information with my colleagues, I was shocked to discover that no one was particularly surprised. "Nancy, you don't care about people's feelings. You are very direct," a fellow colleague explained. "You never seem to care about the story or why something happened the way it did. You just want to move forward without delay." I did deeply care about people, and it troubled me to think that the people around me thought that I didn't. My emotional range was very narrow. I knew happy, sad, anger, and love (more like infatuation). I learned that empathy is the ability to emotionally recognize, understand, and share what other people think and feel. To improve my empathy "score," I needed to increase my own emotional vocabulary and range of expression. One of our branding partners introduced our team to the language of emotion as part of an exercise. There were over one hundred words to express different feelings. From that day on, I have worked to understand my own emotions. While taking that leadership assessment was certainly a humbling experience, I am so grateful to have had it. The truth is, if I had scored higher—say, in the sixtieth or seventieth percentile—I would have decided that it was good enough, and I wouldn't have felt compelled to really change or improve myself.

Several years ago, I took the same assessment again. I was relieved to report that I scored in the eightieth percentile for empathy. While improving from the tenth percentile to the eightieth is a notable improvement, I am still working toward the mastery of empathy in the moment. When I share the story of the first assessment, people are always shocked. This pleases me more than anything else. It's also a good story to share as a leader of high-performing teams because I can use it as an example for other CEOs and leaders to show them that empathy is a skill that can be practiced. I still say "facts, not feelings" and qualify that statement with listen to the story, honor the emotion, and then look at the data to figure out what comes next.

Develop Your Empathy by Developing Your Presence

So much of what empathy is, really, is presence. It's learning to be comfortable enough in the self, in the present moment, to be able to really listen, without judgment or even the desire to fix or solve the problem. It requires a genuine curiosity and interest in other people and their stories. Empathy means listening without involving yourself in the speaker's story. Presence is that grounded self-confidence that allows me to listen without judgment or prescient interest. I practice listening to the story with curiosity, while staying in the moment. From the prior chapter, we've developed the theme that people are the competitive advantage in any company. Self-awareness requires that you focus on your people. How you show up for others, how you manage your energy, and how you connect with the people around you makes all the difference. The relationships that get built between a leader and the team, clients, suppliers, and wider community are the social currency of success.

> **It's the presence of the leader, more than how they dress or walk, that really builds trust and commitment.**

Plenty of books, TED talks, and seminars will tell you the best way to sit, the right way to stand, the proper way to position your body and where to put your hands so that your physical presence matches your leadership style and messaging. These technical details are important to present competence and confidence. The leader must not sacrifice who they are. I am encouraged by a leader who shows up, manages their own energy and the energy of others in the room, and can take in information and process it in the moment. It's the presence of the leader, more than how they dress or walk, that really builds trust and commitment. That presence is what inspires the team to drive toward the mission, the vision, the goals, and the long-term results.

Amy Cuddy, American social psychologist and author, is famous for coining the phrase, "Fake it until you become it." While I understand the training—that you should practice competence, confidence, and the mindset of a more capable person until you are able to embody those qualities—I don't believe in faking it, not for anything or any reason. "You are what you think." Be yourself, be fully present for others, and be vulnerable in the moment, even a moment of discomfort. You don't have to have all the answers, and you certainly don't have to pretend that you do. You just must be alert, curious, and adaptable.

A High-Performance Team Starts with You

Your presence as a leader, more than anything else, dictates the effectiveness of your team. As the leadership goes, so goes the rest of the company. And while the responsibility of this is great, I want to encourage you not to view it as a burden. The trust of your team is a gift and an opportunity to build a high-performance team. It must be something you accept, whole-heartedly, with gratitude and humility. The leader sets the tone!

It's natural for other people to come into meetings with heavy emotions and strong opinions. You can't expect everyone on your team to prioritize calm and presence the way that you, as the leader, must. You are there to receive their energy, to listen with curiosity, compassion, and empathy, and to absorb and transform their energy into something positive and productive. If people on your team feel that they can trust you, they will feel safe enough to speak up and to express doubt or disagreement without fear of repercussions. When people feel safe enough to express their thoughts and feelings in real time without fear of reprisal or judgment, they will speak up and innovate as a trusting team. On the other hand, gossip, and other kinds of expressions of resentment or negativity, can easily fester when people feel the need to express themselves, but don't feel safe doing so in the workspace. When they have a safe container to express doubt or disagreement, even if, in the end, the team decides to go in a different direction, your people will feel heard, knowing that their ideas were respected and their voice was heard.

Be Humble

The data from the "Great Resignation"[17] during the COVID-19 pandemic (2020–2021) has shown us that, more and more, people are refusing to put up with a toxic workplace, or an egotistical boss, even if for a hefty paycheck. More than ever, people are prioritizing a great workplace culture over salary. While companies around the

---

17   Keith Ferrazzi and Mike Clementi, "The Great Resignation Stems from a Great Exploration," *Harvard Business Review*, June 22, 2022, https://hbr.org/2022/06/the-great-resignation-stems-from-a-great-exploration; Bryan Robinson, "Discover the Top 5 Reasons Workers Want to Quit Their Jobs," *Forbes*, May 3, 2022, https://www.forbes.com/sites/bryanrobinson/2022/05/03/discover-the-top-5-reasons-workers-want-to-quit-their-jobs/?sh=222cc7aa5d46; Aaron De Smet, Bonnie Dowling, Bryan Hancock, and Bill Schaninger, "The Great Attrition Is Making Hiring Harder," *McKinsey Quarterly*, July 13, 2022, https://www.mckinsey.com/capabilities/people-and-organizational-performance/our-insights/the-great-attrition-is-making-hiring-harder-are-you-searching-the-right-talent-pools; Kim Parker and Juliana Menasce Horowitz, "Majority of Workers Who Quit a Job in 2021 Cite Low Pay, No Opportunities for Advancement, Feeling Disrespected," Pew Research, March 9, 2022, https://www.pewresearch.org/fact-tank/2022/03/09/majority-of-workers-who-quit-a-job-in-2021-cite-low-pay-no-opportunities-for-advancement-feeling-disrespected/.

globe are suddenly scrambling to retain their workers with perks and bonuses, it's those companies that had already established themselves as having a great workplace environment that were able to retain their employees. In this workplace environment, the "vibe" begins with you.

It's imperative that the leader not lose sight of the reasons for founding the company and assuming the mantle of leadership. Leaning into that vision, the leader must invite the team to commit to the vision as well. A leader who holds too tight to the reins, who makes the decisions by herself, behind closed doors, will never get full buy-in from the rest of the team. The team simply won't have that same sense of ownership. Walking into a meeting with the plans already made is letting ego steer the ship. It's that ego that won't let go of the reins, that won't share the vision, and consequently, that won't share the feeling of success, either, when that vision is realized. An ego like that is palpable. It takes all the air out of the room and takes the enthusiasm with it as well. The ego-driven leader loses out on the most valuable resource in the company: the discussion and questions that inspire and engage the workforce.

Confidence should always be tempered with humility. Humble confidence means that the leader is open to sharing the challenges, as well as the triumphs, and open to advice and recommendations for upgrades. It means that the leader sees and acknowledges the strengths of others. The leader values equally the contributions of the leadership team. Just as people say "I want to surround myself with people who are smarter than me," I would rather say "I want to surround myself with people who have different lived experiences than me and will bring those experiences into the decision-making process." In this way, I am inviting them to use their strengths, and to lead by example. These team members guide me in the aspects of my own leadership, experiences, or knowledge that might need an upgrade. A true leader surrounds herself with people who can see her clearly, warts and all, and those people are invested in helping the company succeed, just as the leader is invested in helping them be the best that they can be as well.

Simon Sinek, author and inspirational speaker, wrote the book *Leaders Eat Last*. Treat every member of the team as though they are the most prized guest at a dinner party and never like someone there to serve a specific purpose. Having humility means not having all the answers, not always being right, and still being accountable. Every member of the team could choose to work somewhere else. But instead, they are present, sharing their skills and expertise in service to the greater vision. Think about it: if you were to invite your guests over for a dinner party, it would be considered extremely rude for you to serve yourself first while your guests waited patiently for you to finish. Being a good leader means making sure, first and foremost, you take care of your people. You want every member of your team to feel that you are putting the company, the issue at hand, the team, and their needs first.

Honor Your Emotions

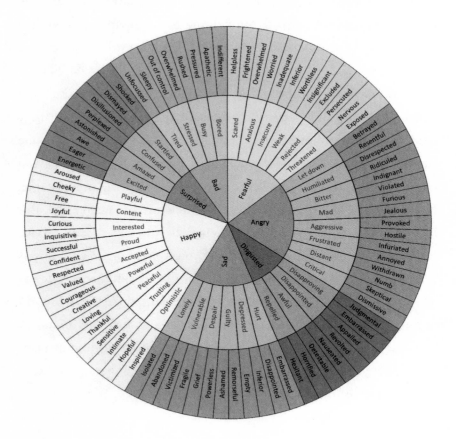

Seeing psychologist Robert Plutchik's wheel of emotions for the first time was mind blowing. There are all these words to really isolate and explain feelings, more precisely. Now, when the faint hue of red begins at my chest bone and works its way up to my cheeks and forehead, I have the language to say "I'm not angry; the emotion I'm feeling is actually something else that's showing up as fear." With this wheel, I can take a beat and label the emotion more specifically. This often happens to me when something triggers that fear in me that I'm not good enough or that I don't have the right answer. Rather than acknowledge my feelings of doubt and insecurity, my mind channels it into what looks like anger, because anger is an easier, more powerful emotion to deal with than fear. At their root, the two most primal, driving emotions are love and fear.

Leadership expert and author Brené Brown has a story in which she realized that she behaves in a "scary" way when she, herself, is in fact, scared. Her story led her to the piece of wisdom "Try to be scared without being scary." It's that same flight or fight mechanism. The critter brain flips on and goes into a defensive mode. When this happens, the only thing one can do is really to interrupt the process by acknowledging the process itself. Fear does not equal danger.

Learning to recognize patterns, identify emotion, and find language for an emotion does wonders to bring those big, scary feelings back down to earth. Adding language to nonverbal cues helps people realize that, though they may feel threatened, though their pulse may be quickening and their breath may be getting short, there is not any true danger. There are no lions or tigers or bears, oh my! It's just a room full of people that they trust, and that trust is going to allow them to work through whatever emotion they feel in a safe place.

I am very fortunate to work with a team who knows me very well. They know what it means when I start to rub my face. For someone else, their lips might purse, or they might cover their mouth to hide an expression. We all have these physical tells, or expressions, that are secretly letting our emotions out, making them visible, whether we are aware of them or not. But a good team will know how to identify and interrupt those processes, to make the unconscious conscious. When my team sees me rubbing my face, they know to ask me a question. They don't have to wait for the explosion. They know to say "What's going on for you? Think it, say it."

As a leader, I, too, have become astute at recognizing people's patterns, so I recognize that feeling of fear, of being threatened or judged. I ask the person to name the emotion (frustrated, stuck, disrespected, scared), bringing the feeling to the surface. The physical expression is necessary when it comes to getting at the root cause that blocks growth. Sometimes there's nothing you can do but fasten your seatbelts and wait out the emotion. Sometimes the physical manifestation is loud and demonstrative, and it's not comfortable to observe. Honoring the emotion means naming it and then releasing the energy and, ultimately, letting go of the story that provokes the threat. It's in these high-risk scenarios, when all the work you've done to build up psychological safety to create trust in low-risk scenarios, pays off. This self-awareness allows for honest conflict to occur, so people can process the issues, not the person. Some teams don't like to use the word *conflict*. It makes them think of yelling and fighting, of out-of-control emotions and passion. If we focus on the issue, not on the person, conflict produces intense discussions that result in creative resolutions. The goal isn't to shame anyone but to debate disparity in experience, process, or analysis. What's going on? How do we get to the bottom of it? Who else do we have to speak to? It's only through this kind of intense focus on the issue, on not shying away from the conflict at hand, that companies grow in terms of focus and scale.

Recognize Your Patterns

Emotions are sticky. They don't want to leave you. They want to stay, lodged in your gut, festering. If you have trouble letting your emotions go, here are a few ideas that can help. Try to concentrate on facts and issues. Ask yourself what happened, rather than how you feel about the event or stimulus. This can help process strong feelings into a calmer place of rationality and recollection. The emotion is the reaction; the response takes effort. First, breathe and honor the emotion. Get control of your breathing, then examine the facts. Focus on the *who* (who did what?), the *what* (what happened?), the *where* (where did this take place?), the *when* (when did it occur?), and the *how* (how did this occur?). As a rule, I like to stay away from questions of why, because *why* responses trigger the threat caused by judgment. Focusing on the more concrete aspects of the conflict moves people's attention away from their emotions, allowing their physical bodies to calm and their feeling of safety to return. It is important to identify and label the trigger and acknowledge the emotion the trigger evokes. As Fred Rogers says, "what is mentionable is manageable."

I have found that when I identify my emotions, honor them in a healthy way, and then refocus my attention on the facts, I am able to determine that the perceived threat is not really a threat at all. I realize I am in a new or unfamiliar experience. It might be that I am overtired because the dogs were up three times last night and I didn't get enough sleep. It might be that I am afraid of being left behind, that I don't matter or don't belong. Learning to identify these triggers does wonders for allowing me to let my defensive posture go. I can truly be present and show up for my teammates as my best self on that day.

Breathing is helpful in settling the energy that gets stirred up by too much emotion. In my experience, telling a person to "Calm down" or "Get hold of yourself" in a moment of high-stakes stress does very little to calm a person down. In fact, it often has the opposite effect. On the other hand, asking open-ended questions redirects the energy to the issue. I often say take a moment and get oxygen to your brain to refocus the attention, which has a direct, calming effect. Breathing exercises are a good way to calm the nerves. I think of breathing as a horizontally expanding exercise, not a vertical one. I like the "Box Breathing" or "Four Square Breathing." This involves inhaling to a count of four, holding air in your lungs for a count of four, then exhaling at the same slow, steady pace, and then holding your breath with lungs empty for another count of four. Then the pattern is repeated three more times. This does wonders to release tension and stress. There are countless other breathing techniques out there, and each one does something slightly different to calm both the body and the mind.

I often conclude a breathing exercise with a question centered around empathy and curiosity. This refocuses the group on the issue and its root cause. Even though one person reacted strongly, it's probable that they weren't the only one who was feeling uncomfortable. They are more like the messenger, pointing out that there is a problem, even before others are even aware of it. So, we don't ignore or patronize the messenger. We acknowledge the courage it takes to be the one to speak up and call us into the issue.

Take Ownership When You Mess Up

When I mess up, I've learned to ask for a do-over. I often teach my clients that, after they calm down, they could start again. Do it once, and that's a good start. But do it twice, and your brain begins to retrain. The brain has amazing plasticity to learn new tasks and train to respond to a stressful situation in a productive and healthy way. That retraining of the trigger response will ultimately become a habit. In addition, the do-over gives everyone in the room an opportunity to end what once was a stressful situation on a high note. To use a sports metaphor: always end on a good note. Make that last free throw before quitting for the day.

One error of judgment isn't going to make or break any company, especially if the team has done the work to develop safety and trust. This feeling of trust extends well beyond the team and applies to the client base as well. If clients are happy with the work the company has been doing, one misstep isn't going to matter much to them. I know—I can speak from experience. As a frequent flier, I've been with United Airlines since the early eighties. While I have seen the company go through its share of CEOs and different strategies, I have stayed loyal because, overall, I am very happy with the service it provides. I remember flying the day that United Airlines and Continental Airlines combined their computer systems. It was an absolute disaster. The computers didn't work, the lines were backed up, and people were fuming. But my loyalty remained unwavering. Why? Because of the prior years of reliable customer service. By the time I got to the front of the line, I approached the distraught United employee, and rather than express my own frustration, I just said "What can I do to make your day better?" I have to say, it felt good, in that moment, to flex that well-exercised empathy muscle.

Practice Presence

My friend, business leader, and author of *The Primes* Chris McGoff outlines a simple mantra: "Be, notice, choose, be." That's it. That's the whole mantra. When I find myself overreacting, I like to repeat this mantra, with lots of silence in between each word, to really give me time to take stock of each stage of the process. I like to think of it this way: First, I just take note of how I'm being. I use a breathing exercise. Then I notice that I do, in fact, have a choice. I can choose to be different in that moment. I ask myself how I want to show up. I make the choice. Finally, I fully embody my choice of being. "You are what you think." And we do, in fact, have the power to think differently and then to be different.

Being fully present, a leader is better equipped for handling those unconscious gestures, facial expressions, and even thoughtless words and actions. Microaggressions, the expression of unconscious bias, are much more likely to slip out when we are tired or hungry or distracted. As we have discussed, over 90 percent of what we communicate comes from nonverbal cues. Our minds process up to ten million pieces of information per second unconsciously. On the other hand, we only process about forty pieces of information at the conscious level.[18] So, at that unconscious level, much is being communicated without our knowledge. If we aren't fully present and in control of our actions, what we are communicating likely isn't the information that we want to convey. If you trust the science, then how you enter a room, your facial expressions, your posture, your hands, your torso, the tone, and the cadence of your voice are sharing more information about you, your beliefs, and your capabilities than you could ever imagine.

Prioritize Self-Care

To show up as your best self, you've got to take care of yourself. These days, "self-care" can mean different things, from getting your nails done to taking a vacation without technology. I focus on energy management.

Managing energy acknowledges that we are social beings with finite resources, including energy and attention. Knowing whether you are an extrovert or an introvert will help you understand how to manage and maintain your energy. (Note: the definition for an

---

18   Pragya Agarwal, *Sway: Unraveling Unconscious Bias* (New York: Bloomsbury Sigma, 2020).

extrovert is someone who gains energy from spending time with other people, while an introvert is someone who gains energy from recovery time alone.) As an introvert, I love being around other people, but by the time that event is over, I am very drained. I need some time alone to recover and refill my energy tank. Other important aspects to energy management include sleep, fuel, hydration, exercise, and time for self-reflection. These are essential to survival and essential to leadership. If I go for too long without a healthy physical and mental practice, I am guaranteed to crash and burn, taking the team down with me. When I've had a bad day and I look back, I realize that I hadn't had enough water, or the right kind of healthy, nutrient filled food, or enough sleep the night before to really prepare me to have my best day. I have noticed that when I eat foods

> **Creating time for self-reflection is the best gift I give myself.**

that are high in salt, carbohydrates, or fats, my energy levels are completely out of whack. Creating time for self-reflection is the best gift I give myself. I recommend finding a routine of exercise, meditation, prayer, and journaling—whatever works as a routine. Being present means taking note of these self-care items and their effect on performance. Self-care means making good choices for yourself.

Use Your Time Wisely

In terms of communication, prioritize person-to-person interactions or at least, screen-to-screen, if in-person meetings aren't possible. All too often I have seen colleagues use email to express big ideas, push big agendas, or express big feelings. While it takes time and energy to craft an email—carefully planning out each, one after the other—emails are still extremely easy to misconstrue. It's easy to read tone into an email, and usually we do it poorly. Use email for logistics, scheduling, sharing information, or requesting action. But save big discussions and decisions for when the group gathers in person. It saves time, and it often saves hurt feelings as well.

Time together is best spent with intentional preparation—the research and reports are done and distributed in advance of the meeting. Participants read and prepare for discussion so that the time in the room together is spent on the decision-making process and not on absorbing the information needed to make the decision. This process requires time and attention to bring the members of the leadership team together for a regularly scheduled meeting to stay aligned on the vision and the priorities of the mission of the business. These meetings bring together the best minds to address issues and make decisions. The leadership's time together is one of, if not *the*, most valuable resources of the business. As a group, the leadership team works on trust and accountability. Team members want to belong, and that means they want to contribute to the cause, acting on behalf of the greater good. Helping people to remember this keeps the mission and the vision at the forefront of the teams' minds.

When teaching communication, I tell leaders "For someone to remember something, they have to hear it seven times." Can you imagine a meeting in which you had to repeat yourself seven times for people to fully take in and understand your point? That would be a nightmare if you had to repeat the same phrase seven times in one meeting. Your team learns in different ways and at different rates. When you repeat something that you said, it encourages them to internalize that information in a new and different way. "Let me restate what I just said to make sure we're on the same page."

Ask for Advice and Commit to Do Better

To become a better leader, the most specific instruction probably isn't in a book. It's likely that the people on the team have quite a few ideas and specific examples for improving your leadership skills. While it takes a degree of humility and bravery to do so, asking questions such as "Could you let me know what's working or not working for you?" and "Can you tell me specifically how I can communicate better?" provides you with a wealth of useful information. It's often better to ask for advice, rather than feedback, as feedback is about what happened in the past, whereas advice is forward facing.

Ask everyone on the team for advice on how to do better in the future, both people who have been with the company a long time and those just starting out. In the military, there is a strategy of always asking the most junior person in the room their thoughts and opinions first. This is to avoid groupthink and the pressure to repeat the same ideas as those in higher-up positions. Because they don't yet know what the rules are, people newer to the team may have a fresh perspective that no one has thought of yet. Finally, it's important to use good listening skills to let your team know they've been heard. Repeat the advice, mirror the language, and then commit to doing better, not just trying. That commitment also includes the invitation to "throw a flag on the play" when the error or omission happens again.

Be Reliable

One of the most important attributes of a leader is reliability. I can't stress this enough. Keep your word as if your life depended on it. Do it within the expected time frame. Show up on time for meetings. Put away the phone. Look at the speaker. Know what you stand for. Go out of the way to make sure every voice on the team is heard, and then decide, stick to it, and see it through. Leadership isn't about consensus; it's about making decisions, and sometimes decision-making is hard. Acknowledge that people on the team have great ideas but that not every idea can be realized. There just isn't enough time in the day, or resources in the world, to make every good idea happen. Be open and honest about the decision-making process; the team will commit if the process is fair and all had the opportunity to speak up. Be honest when you're wrong, with your team and yourself.

Be accountable and give others the permission to hold everyone accountable. Invite that open, honest, and vulnerable communication that is built on trust. And if you behave in a way that's unreliable, own up to it. Be the first to name it, and don't wait to be called out. You don't need to make excuses or take up people's time explaining every mishap that led to your behavior. Simply apologize for it, and do your best to make sure it doesn't happen again.

Be Yourself

I spent so many years trying to be someone else, in so many ways. It took me a long time to figure out who my best self really was. What I discovered was that I wasn't a fancy title or my list of accomplishments. I looked inside and learned to love me just as I am. If there is one thing that you can do to develop that sense of presence that makes a great leader, it's to learn to be, and love, yourself.

The **Takeaways**

1. As goes the leader, so goes the rest of the team.

2. Identify your strengths and your weaknesses and work on both.

3. Do the work to work on yourself, internally and externally.

4. Be accountable and allow others to hold you accountable.

5. Be present to take care of others and yourself.

CHAPTER 4

Your Pipeline

---

*Insanity is doing the same thing over and
over and expecting different results.*
—ALBERT EINSTEIN

Typically, the term "pipeline" in the business world refers to sales. Very few leaders use the same discipline to develop a process for HR. Leaders should deploy the same strategies used in sales to nurture and grow their existing talent team. Finding the right people to put in the right seats is a process that starts with identifying a need, defining a function, developing an applicant pool, hiring the candidate, retaining and training the team member, and creating a career path that has positive results for both the company and the team member. Thinking about the pipeline model for your team builds a succession plan that ensures that the company is, and will be, drawing its strength from committed A players for years to come. Succession and career planning for every person in the organization creates a people-first culture that engages everyone in the future of the business.

What Is a Sales Pipeline?

To be perfectly clear, it's less of a pipe and more of a funnel. The sales funnel provides a good blueprint for a talent pipeline. Companies who are looking to bring in new business begin by casting a very wide net, (1) first taking the time to figure out who and where the prospects are; (2) then finding an introduction to the prospect that identifies if the prospect is within the target market, known as a "warm lead"; (3) and conducting discovery questions based on the common pain points that the product or service might solve (4) before addressing the objections and the factors that contribute to the customer's decision to buy. With good data, a company has identified the right market, the right product, and the right clientele, and the game shifts. The goal is now to repeat the same activities, repeatedly, refining and defining the product or service to ensure that these ideal clients continue to buy.

Within every industry, and every market, success starts as a numbers game. Most salespeople start out with a certain number of calls to make to potential clients. The number of specific activities (that vary by industry and other factors) becomes a predictable number of warm leads, and from there, these warm leads will narrow down to another foreseeable number of actual clients. Once the math has been done, the company only needs to execute the specific activities to get the expected outcome. Think of this as transactional selling. The relationship between buyer and seller culminates in the payment of the invoice.

In the past, sales teams placed emphasis on continually generating new business. However, the focus has shifted to customer experience. We have learned the value of not taking existing clients for granted. We prioritize current clients and customers to entice them into investing deeper into the company, which can mean buying more of the product, innovating to solve new problems, and to refer work to vendors from their networks. As the customer's business grows, they purchase more of the product or services. With each sale, the seller and buyer are building a trusted relationship, identifying new needs, and solving new problems that neither was aware of at the initial stages of the sales pipeline. The "We grow together" approach is a relationship that requires more than delivery of service or goods and payment of an invoice.

From Transaction to Relationship: Customer Experience

It's the added value along the way that makes all the difference in signaling the importance of the relationship to the customer. Paying attention to the little things shows the client that their needs are top of mind. It makes all the difference, especially if that client is a referral source. Filling the pipeline with referrals is the story the client tells others when that extra attention shows up in the buy-sell relationship. That attention to the customer experience takes a commodity transaction and turns it into a relationship.

As a lawyer, I was a client of an expert witness consultancy. Each time I showed up for a meeting, there would be a can of Diet Dr Pepper and a Granny Smith apple. At some point in our business relationship, I must have mentioned that I liked Diet Dr Pepper and Granny Smith apples, because from that point on, I never arrived at a meeting without those two items waiting for me on the conference table. Even my clients who participated in the meetings were welcomed with their favored beverage and snack. I also received birthday cards, including cards for my wife's birthday. These thoughtful actions didn't cost very much, but the little, personal touches showed me that I was a valued client and ensured my loyalty. I regularly told my clients this story when contemplating which service provider to retain. I also referred the company to other lawyers in my firm and other firms. And I learned from the experience. From that point forward, our trial team provided favorite beverage and snack items to our clients during our meetings. These small and personalized gestures start the shift from a mere transaction to a trusted-advisor relationship with our clients.

Taking a commodity transaction to a trusted relationship is a learned skill set. For example, we have lots of choices on where to bank. For the most part, banks offer the same or very similar features. Ultimately, at the end of the day, it's a generic product, a straight commodity transaction. Yet, when I connect directly with my banker, whether personally or digitally, I receive that personal touch that shifts the exchange from a transaction into a relationship. I am greeted personally; we exchange news of our families, and I am asked "How can I help?" It's that added relationship piece that creates customer allegiance and customer loyalty.

Talent Pipelines Put People First

What if leaders expended similar effort and resources to create the feeling of appreciation and attention into the employee relationships? Rather than do the work and get a paycheck, what if the team leader made sure she knew the teams' favorite beverages, who was gluten-free, vegan, or allergic to nuts? Most small businesses lack the resources to provide on-site meals or day care benefits. Yet, the feeling of appreciation and individual attention to the preferences, not just needs, of your employees extends beyond the cost. Putting people first means that you as a leader recognize the individual in the seat across the desk from you and see the person for who he is. Having an employee feel seen and heard means you must see him first before you can hear him.

Developing the talent pipeline requires regular and clear communication in both directions. As a leader, I monitor not only the amount of time I talk, but also how I talk. After settling into the conversation, I ask two questions. "What's working for you? What's not working for you?" I listen carefully and stay curious, asking clarifying questions that do not suggest strategies or solutions. These conversations happen outside the regular meeting schedule and feel spontaneous to the team member. I label these conversations "structured serendipity." By staying curious about the person in the role, I ask about and listen to the goals and dreams of the person. From these conversations, we start work on career development and career goals and discuss how the future works for both the team member and the business.

Learning by Doing

I served as a member of the board of directors of a staffing company for over ten years. During a time of transition, I was asked by the board to serve as interim CEO. This company was in the business of connecting individuals with disabilities with both short and long-term job opportunities. It was a mission in which I believed, and I was happy to take on the new challenge of running the company.

When I stepped into that role, I discovered that the culture of staffing is transactional. The general rule of thumb was that, for every position you filled, a recruiter had to have at least three other people on deck, ready to fill that position when that first employee didn't show up to work that day. People came and went. The jobs were primarily in the food service, landscaping, roadwork, and light healthcare services. Employees from the agency would come in at the end of the week and fill out their hours report, get it signed off on, and receive a check.

The challenge was to think differently about our workforce. To scale, we needed to create a company culture that opened the possibilities of what a person with a disability could do. I began by looking at who was already in the workforce. I realized that probably at least 50 percent of the staff at the agency were individuals with disabilities, who started as part time and temporary employees initially. I decided to give attention to these employees, spread out over a handful of different locations, as if they were our best customers.

> **To scale, we needed to create a company culture that opened the possibilities of what a person with a disability could do.**

I saw and experienced a ripple effect. As these employees felt they mattered to the vision and mission of the company, they began to treat the temporary workers like they, too, were a part of something bigger than just a paycheck at the end of the week. If the goal was to put more individuals with disabilities to work, the leadership team had to create a culture within the organization that wasn't just about the numbers. We wanted our employees to feel proud and passionate about the work, to work in a well-kept environment, to have access to the tools and resources that helped them do the work, and identify career paths that suited their skills and unique abilities. Several members of the leadership team were already practicing these values; they were just doing it without support of the leadership team or the board. As a team, we created the incentives for team members to add value to their clients and their workplace. We celebrated the stories of the relationships that we built, internally and externally. People no longer saw the company as a "temp" agency, a place where they went to pick up their paychecks. Our employees knew that each of them made a difference and learned that the leadership valued the individual and team contributions to the community. Our team members had autonomy, meaning, and purpose. Over time, we changed our title. We were no longer a temp agency, procuring disposable workers for a short period of time for a handful of short-term service jobs. We began calling ourselves a "recruiting agency," one that created relationships by connecting people to longer-term employment that fit both the specific staffing needs of the employer and the skills and needs of the employee.

Hire Differently

By growing our talent and creating career paths, we added diversity to the leadership teams. The executive teams became diverse organically, not because someone had "found" the exact right candidate that checked all the boxes for diversity but because the company itself had invested in, and encouraged, the people it already had on the payroll, grooming them to take on more and more responsibility.

I often hear the statement "We can't find any 'qualified diverse candidates.'" While these leaders claimed to espouse the values of diversity, equity, and inclusion, they were not thinking about their recruiting process as a talent-development process. Time and time again, when there was a position to be filled, the HR manager attended career fairs at the same twenty-five schools or only reviewed résumés that had an uninterrupted employment history. They used the same networks repeatedly. They asked their employees to refer people from their own personal and professional networks, in effect narrowing rather than widening the circle of potential candidates. When it came to hiring, these leaders were looking internally to match the résumés of those already in leadership. Many companies look at the current leaders to confirm that "this is the persona who is successful here."

Of course, we are hard wired to gravitate toward what we know. It's our affinity bias, our confirmation bias, and groupthink, all working together to keep us within our comfort zones. Studies have shown that when sent identical résumés with identical qualifications, if the candidate names are either associated with women or African American culture, then those candidates are 30–50 percent less likely to receive a call back.[19] When it comes to filling the talent pipeline, to finding diverse talent, and to creating a succession plan that brings in diverse talent and nurtures the talent already in the system, we absolutely must break our old habits and do things differently. We must think outside of the box. We must fish in a different pond.

A word of warning, however: None of this happens by flipping a switch. A 180-degree turn to move away from the things and the people that have worked for decades is frightening. Moving too far, too quickly, from the core recruiting model without intention and attention, may also damage the business. Move intentionally, expanding in concentric circles outside of the core. This is really what growing a diverse talent pipeline is all about. It's about going after a different customer and a different type of applicant. Doing the same thing for years, decades even, requires a communication strategy that helps the culture change and work toward psychological safety within the old framework. It really is a delicate dance of extending out the

---

19   "Women are 30 Percent Less Likely to Be Considered for a Hiring Process than Men," Phys.org, March 26, 2019, https://phys.org/news/2019-03-women-percent-hiring-men.html; Marianne Bertrand and Sendhil Mullainathan, "Are Emily and Greg More Employable than Lakisha and Jamal?" June 20, 2024, https://scholar.harvard.edu/files/sendhil/files/are_emily_and_greg_more_employable_than_lakisha_and_jamal.pdf.

core and communicating the purpose and meaning of change while still staying true to the values of the team.

Show You Care from the Very Beginning

In times of low unemployment and a slow job market, employees will move for a career that gives them autonomy, meaning, and purpose. In the Great Resignation and the quiet quitting movement, many knowledge workers are looking to get away from a toxic work environment, to have flexibility, and to be appreciated for their skills. Strong employment relationships put people first, recognizing the person who produces the results rather than someone who "clocks in for the job." This attitude among jobseekers is an advantage for the company that values people as well as profit.

For efficiency, many companies use technology to sift through the early round of résumé reviews. This can make the experience of applying for a job an extremely impersonal, transactional experience. Often, prospective applicants will carefully craft a cover letter and polish up their résumé, only to receive not so much as an acknowledgment of the application from the employer. While this kind of "ghosting" is common practice these days, it also means that going against the grain will ensure that a company stands out as a much more caring and attentive employer. Just the simple act of sending out an acknowledgment of receipt of the application to every person who applies, as well as a letter of rejection with a thank you for applying, distinguishes most companies from its industry competitors.

Fish in a New Pond

Great leadership is more afraid of the status quo than of change. "If you're not growing, you're dying." To diversify the talent in the organization, the company must stop using the same process and recruit in new places with different expectations. HBCUs (historically Black colleges and universities), such as Spelman University in Atlanta and Howard University in Washington DC, are turning out extraordinary individuals prepared to do extraordinary things. There are numerous other HBCUs that don't get the attention they deserve. Prioritize going to these campuses, work with their career offices, and ask questions about becoming an ideal company to attract their top talented students. The good news is that students from these schools are getting more offers, more interviews, and more opportunities as more companies commit to a diverse workforce. The bad news for companies is that means more competition in attracting those talented, and often overlooked, candidates. Recruiting for mid- and senior-level positions also requires new processes for finding and vetting candidates. There is no "perfect" résumé. There are candidates whose careers have taken interesting turns that are worth the time and effort to discover. It takes more time, attention, energy, and resources to find candidates that share the core values, are passionate about the mission and purpose of the company, and bring lived experiences to improve the decision-making process.

Expand the Definition of Potential

It's not enough to simply recruit for new talent. The metrics to evaluate these applicants must evolve as well. More and more, leaders are coming to understand that a wealth of diverse lived experiences prepares an applicant to excel in a job just as much as a degree from a "top" university. This means reexamining the systems that we use to evaluate applicants. Ask these questions: What are the attributes that are required to do this role well? What are the behaviors? What are the functions and skill sets needed? Thinking deeply about these questions serves the company much better than simply looking for a grade point average from a prestigious university and résumé highlights.

When I was first applying to work at the UN, I was flown all the way to Geneva for the testing and interview portion of the application. After an intense round of interviews, I was brought into a small room and was asked to take a written test. About a week before, I had received a thick stack of materials in preparation. Even though I was jet-lagged, I had a clear idea that what was being tested was more than just my writing skills. Like so many assessments, there was no "right" answer. The assessment focused on my analytical skills, as well as my communication skills. In essence, could I do the very simple thing of following the instructions I had been given, namely, to read the materials. I will always remember that skills test, and thought it was a very good model for applications of all sorts. No right answers, no trick questions. Was I able to follow directions.

When reading stacks of résumés and cover letters, my eyes glaze over after the first thirty minutes. I start to notice the things that are most apparent. Who has taken the time and care to format their résumé so that there is a nice balance of text and white space? Who has chosen a font that is pleasing to the eye? Who has made sure that there are no spelling or punctuation errors or typos in their documents? Who uses the brief few paragraphs of their cover letter to concisely share as much pertinent information about themselves, without excess? Even before I set about to dig into the question of who these people are and what their experience is, there is so much to be gleaned from just these things. It's these little things that show attention to detail and for polish in a final product. That said, a perfectly crafted résumé does not guarantee that the person sitting across from me is the right candidate for the job. I check my bias as I review a résumé, looking to match the person to the function and role of the position. I look for the story that opens the door to an interview about whether the person sitting with me is the same as the person on the page.

Use Assessments to Your Advantage

There are many assessments to help employers find the best applicant for the job and to match current employees with positions that fit their skill sets. My favorite is talent optimization from Predictive Index. This assessment was developed over six decades ago by Arnold Daniels, a member of the US Army Corps who began studying what made successful teams work. Over time, this index has been revised and refined, and thousands of companies have used the index to measure behavioral drives (identified as dominance, extraversion, patience, and formality) in addition to cognitive ability. This test takes approximately six minutes to complete and is excellent at predicting a person's workplace behavior, as well as identifying what role they will fulfill within a team context.

There are many other assessments that are valuable resources for identifying ideal applicants and creating well balanced, functional teams. For example, there are the Kolbe Indices (Fact-Finding, Follow Through, Quick Start, Implementer), which are assessment tools that help individuals and teams understand the ways that individuals and their teams use energy, work together, and communicate effectively. There are also assessments that help define behavioral characteristics, to best help your employees understand themselves, the ways they learn, work, and grow and how they fit in a team. A few good examples of this are the DiSC styles (*D* stands for *dominance*, *I* for *influence*, *S* for *steadiness*, and *C* stands for *conscientiousness*) or the Myers-Briggs Type Indicator (extraversion/introversion, sensing/intuition, thinking/feeling, judgment/perception), which identifies the ways that people perceive the world and make decisions. I also am a fan of Gallup's StrengthsFinder and Patrick Lencioni's Working Genius.

These assessments don't remove bias completely. They simply identify strengths, skills, and characteristics. Someone who would be terrible at one job may be well suited in a complementary position. There is no way to "fail" any of these "tests"; there are only ideal matches and less-than-ideal matches. I have found these assessments to be invaluable resources for creating teams that are diverse, not only in their backgrounds but in their skills and approach to problem-solving.

Know the Job

The job title or description on the job board is not the same as the function and the role. The most effective way of understanding the function is by asking the person currently doing the job to track their activities. Recording the activities in a log every fifteen minutes is a great way to understand, in detail, the components and activities for success. After delineating the function and the role, match the competencies, skills, and core values to the job description. From a diversity perspective, do away with requirements that are not correlative to the actual job. Not every position requires a four-year college degree. Finally, no two people will do the job or perform the same way to achieve the desired results.

For internal postings, it's helpful to have a person make a list that identifies the activities at which they excel and the things they love doing. If many of the activities that take up so much of a person's daily tasks aren't in at least one of these two categories (it's ideal if many of the things are in both!), rest assured that this person's time and talent are being wasted. If this is an employee whom you otherwise love, who fits with your core values, see if you can find a role for them that fits their passions so they can be their best self every day.

Keep Your People

It's one thing to get someone in the front door, but it's a whole different ball game when it comes to keeping them. Good employees are going to know their own worth, and consequently, they are going to be highly desirable to other companies. So how do you keep these A players at the company?

If the team is diverse at the entry level and does not advance with a defined career path, the senior-level leadership is unlikely to represent many lived experiences or identities.

If the team is diverse at the entry level and does not advance with a defined career path, the senior-level leadership is unlikely to represent many lived experiences or identities. If the company is not showing interest in these team members, particularly those talented folks who haven't taken the "traditional" path to leadership, they aren't going to stay with the company long term. Have managers hold one-to-one meetings with every team member. Structure the meetings to be a conversation between the two and teach the manager to ask questions about what's working or not working, about career path and opportunities, and about individual goals and personal achievement. Create a shout-out program that shows appreciation for leaning into the core values and extraordinary contributions. Celebrate the promotions and years served. Reward team members with special gifts for their contributions to the company success.

When thinking about how to retain customers and clients, we have learned to provide them with adjacencies—supplemental complimentary products or services that they will need to grow their business. We should really be doing the same with our employees as well. This goes back to treating your team members like guests at your dinner party. Make sure they have a competitive benefits package, as well as room for professional and personal growth. Help them map out a career plan. Give them the opportunity to take a sabbatical and pay for them to go to conferences and workshops. All these experiences will develop the team both personally and professionally so that they can bring back what they have learned and apply it in the workplace.

Create Opportunities

There is nothing more damaging to morale within a company than continuously hiring for the executive positions from the outside. In effect, the team is learning in real time that there are very few, if any, growth opportunities for them in the company. Hiring from the outside, even if a candidate has the "perfect" credentials and checks a box for diversity, sends a confusing message to the career team member, the knowledge workers, and midlevel managers. The tension to diversify the senior teams and to grow organic leaders remains a difficult conundrum. Without engaging the leadership team in discussions about dueling "right actions," two competing goals, a leader might destroy the work done to promote the idea that you see and hear your team members and that you care about them and their development in the company.

I work with clients who will point to the diversity of talent they have in the warehouse or on the shop floor. Sometimes the middle management reflects a myriad of backgrounds and experiences, and some of those managers have moved up from lower levels, but from that point on, career opportunities level off. There seems to be a ceiling that middle management hits, and then executives are brought in almost exclusively from the outside. Developing middle managers is giving them resources (time, attention, continuing education, and apprenticeship) to follow their passions, which may result in a new career at a different organization.

Most leadership teams want to make a difference in diversity at the senior level, essentially creating a mirror of the demographics of their organization and community. They do the work to educate themselves, read books, and participate in diversity trainings. But every time a position opens at the senior vice president level or higher, the instinct is to hire from the outside. For all the talk of fishing in different ponds, I am surprised at how many companies don't think to go fishing right in their own backyard, which sometimes has the most diverse and experienced "fish" one can find. Who better knows the company, inside and out, than the people who have moved through various positions and understand the way the whole system functions? They have direct relationships with those doing the work in various functions and have gathered the trust and respect of their peers through real relationship building. A culture of equity and inclusion closes the career gap and creates opportunities for growth for team members.

In this current environment, organizations are looking to hire for a new function in the C-suite. The titles vary from chief diversity officer to chief people officer. The first instinct is to hire someone, often a person of color, from outside the organization who may or may not have experience in building a culture of inclusivity yet certainly has the lived experiences in a company setting to understand the systemic effects of inequality in the workplace. While this is a well-meaning instinct, all too often, the new hire is not given the resources, including time and attention, to effectively lead the diversity effort. Despite their effort, they have no staff, no budget, and no voice at the executive table. They have been hired as a quick fix to a deep and systemic problem and not given time to learn how things work, inside and out. The reality is that the journey toward a functioning equity and inclusion model isn't something that can be fixed quickly. It takes three to five years of concerted, conscious effort to transform company culture.

Therefore, it's so important to know your people, really know them, from the shop floor to the executive boardroom. Take the time to learn what people are curious about and what they care about. What unique attributes and skill sets do they have that differentiate them from one another? Be in the habit of hiring for the long term, not just with the idea of fulfilling a single role but imagining a future career for the candidate. Hire people who have the potential for not one but two promotions. Find those people who want to be creative and curious, who want to learn and grow their skills, staying strategic and laser focused. People coming straight out of college might not have such a clear idea of what they want to do with their lives, so it's important to prompt them to envision their future. After a couple of years at the company, ask about their perfect job. "In five or ten years, where do you see yourself? What did you do five years ago to begin that process that brought you here?" As a leader, be interested in their passions and goals. Part of the experience of being a beginner is learning about oneself. And part of the role as a leader is helping them to do just that.

Even if that employee leaves the company after a year or so, it's a leader's responsibility to help them grow, regardless of whether it's at the company or elsewhere. The hard truth is they may determine that another company is a better fit for them. Leaders support every team member to be their best selves.

Know Your People

As a leader in the organization, it's your responsibility to model relationship building. There is nothing more impactful than knowing the name of everyone with whom you interact. It doesn't take much, just a few little personal details about each person, much like we do with our best clients. For remote and virtual teams, a simple ten-minute phone call or a quick message lets the team know you care. Make sure to ask them both about what's working, as well as what's not working. Ask questions such as "What's going on? I noticed you did something great. What did you do there?" or "I noticed something didn't work out so well. What do you think we should have done differently? What should you have done differently?" These little check-ins, when they are done with a mindset of curiosity and empathy, not judgment and criticism, earn the trust of the team because they feel seen, heard, and supported.

In every company in which I have worked, I made it a point to walk the "floors" on a regular basis. I knew most of the people with whom I worked, even when we were on different floors. There were days when my hands were smudged with ink because I had stopped to help the IT person change the toner in the copy machine while I was waiting for my document to print. I learned that when a person in a position of power participates and pays attention, the team starts to model the same behaviors. The appreciation, kindness, and gratitude get noticed by many. Such attention can't be faked or phony. It's about taking the time and effort to get to know everyone in the work environment and making genuine relationships.

Give of Yourself

All this connection and relationship building is only possible if the leader is comfortable enough to be vulnerable and accessible. It might not come easily to share a story about the weekend's activities. (I admit it took me many years to be able to do this. I hated sharing personal information about myself!) Time and attention are valuable gifts that return much for the cost of the investment. Lead the company by example; create a culture of vulnerability, care, curiosity, and empathy. Create a culture that people will want to be a part of, to invest in, and to commit to.

The **Takeaways**

1. Building a talent pipeline is a process that is relationship based, not transactional.

2. Reexamine your bias about the places from which you can find talent.

3. Developing talent is a two-way conversation that works best when you ask questions rather than tell stories.

4. Say please and thank you, and listen with all your senses.

5. Show you care with your time and attention.

CHAPTER 5

Your Profits

What gets measured gets managed.
—PETER DRUCKER

At the end of the day, the business must be profitable to stay open and achieve the vision. Otherwise, you have a hobby or a charitable foundation. A successful business considers its market, prioritizes its activities to generate revenue, and ultimately, distributes money to its owners. It doesn't matter how inclusive, conscientious, or considerate the company culture is: if the business doesn't turn a profit, the company closes. Luckily, in recent years, a multitude of studies have come out with ample data that irrefutably points to the fact that having a diverse workforce improves profitability.

Creating a workplace in which people feel seen and heard, have different lived experiences as well as a diversity of thought and thought processes, is actually a help rather than a hindrance to the bottom line. While there is all kinds of data that we can point to in order to prove that equity and inclusion in the workplace is a competitive advantage in business, the quote above sums up the ethos of the sentiment.

People Are the Competitive Advantage

As Bob Dylan sang, "The times, they are a changing," and the American workforce is changing right along with it. In 2020, 67 percent of the US workforce was between the ages of twenty-one and fifty-two. This means that the current workforce is more diverse in terms of age, experience, and ethnicity, than ever before. Much of this workforce is still in their twenties and thirties, and they want and expect a diverse workplace with an inclusive culture. Studies have also shown that 60 percent of people who were born in Generation X and the millennial generation think it's important to support brands that have diverse leadership and invest in social causes. According to recent studies from Pew Research in 2017[20] and McKinsey in 2020, the more diverse your group of leaders in management or the individuals who make up your think tank, the faster you're going to grow your revenues. For example, when it comes to gender diversity, studies show that if you have gender diversity in your leadership, you are likely to experience a whopping 25 percent increase in profitability over a comparable company that doesn't have gender equity in their workplace.

As for hiring a workplace that is differently abled, a report conducted in 2018 by Accenture[21] found that companies that have a leadership team with one or more individuals who self-identify as having a disability are four times more likely to increase ownership or shareholder value than those who do not have anyone with a disability

---

20   Pew Research, 2017; Hunt, Prince, Dixon-Fyle, and Yee, "Delivering through Diversity."

21   "Getting to Equal: The Disability Inclusion Advantage," Accenture.

on their leadership team. Lastly, when we talk about cultural or ethnic diversity, according to a study reported on by *Harvard Business Review* in 2018,[22] if you have a culturally diverse workforce, you are more likely to outperform your peers by 36 percent. And when it comes to innovation, if you have a diverse leadership team, you are 70 percent more likely to report that you have captured a new market. The proof is in the data. Any way you slice it, the reality is that diversity is good for your people, your employees, and your customers—and your bottom line as well.

Financial Literacy

I will be the first one to admit that when someone enters the room and starts talking about numbers, my eyes roll back in my head. I am quite envious of those business owners who were trained with a background in accounting. Although I do know how to read a profit and loss statement and the importance of cash flow, this part of running a business requires attention. I joke sometimes that when it comes time to crunch numbers, my accountants give me the oversize calculator, the one with the big buttons. Every entrepreneur must develop financial literacy to succeed in the business world.

Watch Your Money

Regardless of whose money has been invested in your company, whether it's a financial institution, an angel investor, or your own personal investment, the leaders have a responsibility to understand and report on their financial position and prepare financial reports at

---

22 Lorenzo and Reeves, "How and Where Diversity Drives Financial Performance."

least quarterly and possibly monthly. That said, I look at our cash position every day. Get in the habit of looking at your bank statement at the end of each day. Look at your credit statements and your loan statements. If it causes you discomfort to be so focused on money, well, that's good! Hopefully it will also keep you motivated as well.

> **The business owner must accept responsibility for the numbers and should be well versed in the financial status of the company.**

The business owner must accept responsibility for the numbers and should be well versed in the financial status of the company, even if the company has an accountant, controller, or chief financial officer. "What's the daily balance?" or "How are we doing on sales?" The business owner must know these critical numbers like she knows her birthdate. And she must understand their significance to the operations of the business. A business cannot manage profitability by managing expenses. It's all about the revenue.

The Various Forms of Profit

In its simplest form, having a profit just means that your business earned more money in revenue than it spent to deliver the services and products and to pay its employees and keep the lights on. Of course, when we start to break down the finer points of profit, things can get a little bit trickier. Let's break down the three kinds of profit for you—gross profit, operating profit, and net profits (also sometimes referred to as *the bottom line*).

Gross Profit

Generally defined, gross profit is the sale minus the cost of the goods or services (also sometimes referred to as *COGS*) used to create the product or service. Gross profit takes into consideration the cost of the direct material goods as well as the direct labor that goes into creating the product. The gross profit number doesn't factor in many of the other line items necessary to operating the company, like payroll, monthly rent for the office and warehouse, or the marketing budget. The gross profit number tells you whether the price paid by the buyer is greater than the material cost and direct labor cost to make and deliver the product or service.

Operating Profit

The second number that you need to know is the operating profit. This is the money that is left over after deducting for the costs to operate your business. These operating costs might be fixed costs, meaning the expense is the same every month, or variable costs, meaning the expense is likely different each month. Fixed costs are those that will stay predictable and, for the most part, the same, month after month—rent and insurance—while variable costs are those costs that are more likely to fluctuate—shipping costs, payroll, utilities, travel expenses, and marketing costs. The operating cost is also where things start to get complicated, in terms of the line items that get included. The purpose of keeping track of the operating profit is to have a clear view of how the company is allocating its financial resources so that the expenses to run the business are less than the gross profit number.

Net Profit

The third number is the net profit. This, ultimately, is the bottom line. It's the money that is left over at the end of the day for distribution to the owners, to reinvest into the business, and for profit sharing with the team. It's the residual money after all deductions as well as anything added or deducted, such as interest earned and taxes paid. This, ultimately, is the most important metric for gauging whether your business is sustainable, scalable, and attractive to a future owner.

Why It Matters

If you are interested in scaling the business, the leadership must review each of these profit numbers monthly. The bank's credit officer will want to see these numbers in an organized manner. Lenders want to see that the business has gross profits, that it has room to grow, and that it will be able to pay back the debt that accrues with them. Even if the net profits, the bottom line, is still in the red (not making a profit), if the gross profit and the operating profit are in the black (making a profit) the business has a shot at getting additional funds for growth. Institutional lenders review the history of cash flow and profitability and seldomly lend on projections. Remember, the ability to secure and utilize other people's money is how a business grows, so it's imperative that lenders work with a leader they trust and a company that has a future.

Where to Learn More

If you need more information about how to put together an income statement, or a profit and loss statement, the website for the United

States Small Business Administration (www.sba.gov) is an excellent resource. Another resource is your regional Community Development Financial Institution program (www.cdfifund.gov). Each institution has a wealth of learning modules on financial literacy, many of which are in video form. In addition, they also have templates for spreadsheets you can use, as well as information for learning more about the three profit categories.

Pay Attention to Your Cash Flow

In a small or midsize business, cash is king. You must know your cash position every day. Not every month, not even every week, but every single day. You need to know how much cash is available, not just what's in the bank (because that money could be earmarked already for expenses). Pay close attention to how much money is coming in and how much is going out. What are the trends on a monthly or an annual basis? This is the information that will indicate whether the business is scaling up, adding more people, more products, and more services to the roster.

Seeing a negative number on the cash flow statement is not a cause for panic. There are several reasons in a particular month that you spent some of that excess cash to grow. Or perhaps there are uncollected receivables that haven't made it into the bank just yet. It is normal to have a few months in the red, but it requires investigation, particularly if there is a new service offering or new market expansion.

As a founder and business owner with no accounting background, I use the cash flow statement to observe the trends over time and to determine just how well the business is performing. If the cash flow is static—maybe we gain a little, or we lose a little each month—we aren't growing. That tells me that we've got to tweak something. We either need to grow more revenue, or we've got to reduce the cost of goods and expenses. If the statements don't show a clear potential for growth, potential investors are unlikely to fund the business. Presenting reliable financial statements coupled with the confidence of an owner who has a finger on the pulse of the market signals that the business has the capability to scale.

I subscribe to the adage that "if you are not growing the business, the business is dying a slow, inevitable death." That said, there are business owners who don't want to grow for growth's sake. More and more, these types of businesses are set on maintaining a sustainable, manageable amount of business. These businesses are intentional about their sustainability and stay profitable without trying to scale to sell as an exit plan. However, if the planned exit is to sell the business to the employees, to a competitor, or even to a client, then it's important to demonstrate the potential value of the company, because a buyer looks at the company as an asset that will return a profit on the investment over time.

Many start-ups self-fund with loans to the company. The promissory note is often set up to pay back principal and interest over time several years out. The company carries the debt on the balance sheet. This type of investment is different from equity or shareholder value. The documentation must be correct from the start of the business. Self-funding is a great way to show future investors that they are looking at a well-managed, well-cared-for company.

Stay Leaner Longer

In the early stages of a new business, I remind myself that growth is often three steps forward and two steps back, which still counts as one step forward. There is a constant need to make small adjustments, to keep tweaking and refining. My business advisor, Professor Lynda Applegate, counsels to be smart and patient with the investment of money and time. In every stage of business, every penny counts. Starting a business, beta testing the product or service, and piloting the program at the lowest projected budgets reduces the risk of losing your financial investment. Continue testing the product with new clients and seek input, advice, and recommendations for improvement. Make sure that it is attractive to the customer base at a price point that is within their budget.

The Tale of the Taco Truck

Every day for lunch, a whole host of food trucks would show up in the office building parking lot to serve the employees in the nearby buildings. But Tuesdays were special. "Taco Truck Tuesday" meant live music and family-recipe tacos instead of burgers or a brown-bag lunch.

The taco truck sat nestled between the fried chicken truck, shawarma truck, and the beef slider truck. The line for the taco truck was always the longest. People would spend a half an hour patiently waiting in line just to get their tacos. And I was certainly one of them. While I waited, I chatted with the server who would take our orders while we waited in line. He learned our names, knew our regular orders, and offered to get us our drinks while we waited. One afternoon, I struck up a conversation with the owner of the taco truck. When I asked him about how his business was going, he confessed to me that, despite appearances, he was struggling financially. He just couldn't understand it. His truck was the most popular one in the whole parking lot. His bank account was shrinking while trying to make a go of his taco truck; he just couldn't seem to break even.

Now, I may not have a degree in accounting, but I had been involved in business for some time at this point. So, I asked him how he decided to charge three dollars per taco. He confessed that he just made that number up, based on what he thought people would be willing to pay. I asked him how much it cost to make a single taco. He explained that, because he bought all his ingredients and his materials in bulk, he really had no idea how much it cost to make a taco. So we did the math on the back of a napkin to estimate the cost of a single taco. He included all the ingredients: the meat, the cheeses, the veggies, the shells, and the spices, and he included the paper baskets and the little pieces of paper on which the tacos were served. It was simple arithmetic that even a lawyer with a big-button calculator could figure it out. This was his magic number, because he would know the cost to make a batch of tacos and, with some simple arithmetic, the cost to make a single taco.

The next time I spoke with the owner, he exclaimed, "You aren't going to believe this, but it costs me three dollars and fifty cents to make a single taco. So even before labor, even before the cost of the truck and the fuel and the permits, I lose twenty-five cents every time I sell a taco!" (This, of course, was his gross profit, which was a red number.) He continued, "I kept thinking that if I just kept selling more and more tacos, I would eventually start to turn a profit, but now I realize that the more tacos I sell, the more money I'll lose!"

He told me that he knew he had no choice but to raise his prices or he'd be out of business very soon. But he was afraid that raising his prices would mean losing his customers. Maybe people wouldn't want to pay the amount it would cost to really make a taco. Maybe that thirty-minute line would shrink to a mere fifteen-minute wait. His tacos were the best lunch item in the parking lot. He had worked hard to make friends with everyone in his line and had built up a loyal customer base, person by person.

He had to consider how much to raise his prices. He had to charge at least three dollars and fifty cents to break even on his ingredients, but this didn't factor in all the other expenses like paying his employees and servicing his truck. Ultimately, he ended up raising his prices to four dollars and fifty cents per taco. But the surprising thing was, after a few months, not only did his revenue increase but the wait for his tacos had also increased to forty-five minutes. He realized he could sell more tacos at a higher price because people wanted his product and were willing to pay more.

Sadly, this is where the story takes a turn. This family business was finally making money. His business was finally sustainable and growing. He had figured out his expenses and at last had the money to hire an accountant to handle all the financial details. He even invested in a few iPads to make payment much faster, so that the business no longer had to be cash only. Every detail that went into his business was about serving his customer. They began to do so well with their business that he decided he would take that revenue and invest in a second taco truck. He wanted to scale up.

For his second taco truck, he used a very similar model to the one that had worked so well for him with the first truck. The only thing he changed was the location. Instead of a parking lot in Palo Alto, he positioned this new truck in a parking lot in Mountain View, just a few miles south of the first. But inexplicably, he just wasn't making any money on his second taco truck. He told me he couldn't figure it out. He had the same model—same great tacos, same family recipe, same price point, and a very similar target market—but for some reason the people weren't interested in his tacos in Mountain View.

Well, after some investigation, it turned out that what he didn't have in his new location was that same great customer service. In his new location, the server he had hired didn't really attend to the customers as carefully as the one he had in Palo Alto. They didn't bother to learn everyone's names, offer to get them drinks, or make the wait for their tacos more enjoyable. What he learned from this process was that it's not just the price point or the quality of his tacos but also his customer service. He learned that profits aren't just driven by the quality of the product but are also influenced by the individual relationships that you build, over time, with your customers.

For every business, whether it's banking, real estate, or tacos, there's a transaction or a relationship. Each of those businesses engage in transactions, but the profits don't come simply from selling the product or service for more than their cost. Profits, especially net profits that end up in the owner's pocket, are the result of the relationships that build over time in the business. Now that I can deposit a check online, I could be a client of almost any bank in the world. But what makes me stay with my local bank is the customer service that I get from "my banker" who greets me personally, meets my needs, says please and thank you, and asks if there is anything else without trying to sell me a product.

> **Profits are the result of the relationships that build over time in the business.**

Client Service

More than ever before, clients are now expecting to see that the brands that they buy are invested in them and their communities. Clients want to support companies who have people in leadership who look like them. Showing that you are invested in improving the lives of the communities that are made up of the customers you serve is one of the main things that creates loyalty.

Having great leadership and management who look like and reflect the interest and needs of the customer base increases the likelihood of great customer service, which results in brand loyalty. People drive profits. The employees who feel their voices are heard and their contributions matter will build relationships with customers. Maximizing the equity and inclusion efforts with the team at every level of the business drives profits.

Perfect Your Systems

I advise a start-up that tries to get better food and better services to underserved neighborhoods. We do this by working with inner city business districts, their businesses, and their members. We know that the product is excellent. We have a proof of concept in place, technology that works, and a demand from different nonprofit organizations who want to use the product. The next step is to attract investors to fund growth to serve new communities. In the beta test, the company operated in several cities in the same state. The numbers grew faster than projections. However, expanding the services to two adjacent states did not work according to projections. Investors who had previously showed interest indicated concern for the ability to scale.

At a recent leadership meeting, it became clear that implementation of the strategy by the operations team was not supporting the expected growth. The leadership team revised the strategy and pulled back from the new geographies, which admittedly, sounds quite counterintuitive. The revised strategy, instead, was to stay put and do the same thing, repeatedly, in the same place, until they have proven that this is not just a product that works but that it's a product that people want to buy over the long term. The start-up had to slow down and focus on perfecting the sales and marketing process before expanding. Staying leaner longer really means focusing on the core services within one target market. Staying focused on your core goods and services, with your core customer market, and building up that income over time to then invest your net profits into the next phase of business is really the secret to predictable, sustainable growth.

Be a Data Geek

Going slow to go fast is a means to growing the business in a responsible and sustainable way. Look at the challenges with the lens of an outsider. Create a weekly dashboard or scorecard that reports both financial and forward-looking activities that are correlated to revenue and expenses. These forward-looking activities are the key performance indicators (KPIs) that track the trends in the business. Use both forward-looking and historical measurables. Tracking relevant performance data on a weekly basis allows the leadership team to make corrections early when a process is not working. Collect the data about both revenue-generating and expense activities. Be deliberate with decision-making to do more of the activities that are working and producing gross and net profits. Make small corrections along the road to sustainability (operating profits) and eventually to scalability (net profits).

Understanding how the money flows is imperative to building a scalable business. There are numbers to be crunched and markers to track. Remember, gross profits and operating profits are there to indicate that your business has growth potential. Net profit indicates how much is going to be going into your own pocket and whether there are enough reserves to invest in growth, whether that expansion is into additional products or services, different markets, different demographics, or different regions.

It doesn't matter whether the industry is financial, manufacturing, professional services, or logistics, every business is a commodity if there isn't attention to the customer experience. The attention to the financials is the activity that increases the odds that the business will grow and achieve its mission. Create a dashboard that tracks the activities that generate revenue and tracks financial performance on a weekly basis.

The **Takeaways**

1. Know your cash position; check your bank accounts daily.

2. Even if you're not a "numbers" person, understand the basics of your profit and loss statements.

3. Develop a dashboard that tracks your finances and the key performance indicators to track trends.

4. Develop, upgrade, and maintain routine financial reporting processes.

5. Develop an intentional customer experience process.

CHAPTER 6

Your Partners

If you want to go fast, go alone. But if you want to go far, go together.
—AFRICAN PROVERB

A partnership, by definition, is an arrangement where two or more parties agree to cooperate to advance their mutual interests. A partnership is reciprocal. It must be exactly and delicately fair, not equal, in terms of resources, energy, money, skills, and open and honest communication. The ideal partners are 100 percent aligned on sharing a vision and a passion for what they are doing and where they are going.

A partnership can exist in many kinds of relationships, from the purely transactional and networking relationships to our closest family members and spouses. Partnership is time, energy, property, skill sets, mentorship, sponsorship, networking, and support—and it's also friendship.

I like to imagine that a partnership, in its essence, is two (or more) people standing both shoulder to shoulder and back to back. Imagine a cop film in which the two buddies sit in the vehicle sharing laughs and stories, then a moment later standing back to back, each one making sure the other doesn't get caught by surprise. More than two partners will widen the circle, from three to two hundred, but the idea of protecting the shared mission, shared goal, and shared resources stays the same. These are coconspirators, driving for the same result. There is trust and psychological safety, such that each partner is committed to being challenged, being curious, and exploring how to be the best version of themselves. This kind of relationship, at the core of any business, will have a ripple effect, serving as a model for all the dynamics and relationships in a company. This is culture.

As Chris McGoff states in his book *The Primes*, a good business partnership allows you to open to the possibility of wearing your "big hat" as opposed to your "little hat" when approaching business relationships. As he defines it, your "big hat" is the one that oversees and considers the whole of the organization or company, whereas the "little hat" is more narrowly focused on the good of the department or the individual. While different circumstances certainly call for different hats, I have found that a good partnership is one that allows you to keep your focus on the big picture and not to get stuck in the weeds. Among partners, there must be one who wears the "big hat" when there is not agreement on the decision that must be made. An inclusive and equitable culture leans into conflict, expressing ideas, thoughts, and opinions without ego and then making the decision that all will commit to the course of action because all have been heard. In effect, culture encourages you to wear your "big hat" and make decisions about what's best for the mission, the passion, the company, and the partnership.

Be There for Your Partner

About twenty years ago, I was at a conference put on by a peer-networking organization of women CEOs. The keynote speaker that year was Jim Collins, business author and consultant, and after his speech, I attended a small group lunch with Collins. He had just put out his book *Good to Great: Why Some Companies Make the Leap and Others Don't.* Collins described his research methods for studying what makes or breaks a successful company. The story with the greatest impact on me that day was about rock climbing. Collins is from Colorado and is an avid rock climber, and what he described that day, the scaling of the jagged wall of rocks with little more than a rope and some flimsy metal attachments, was a perfect metaphor for a business relationship. While it may have sounded dramatic, the truth was if one of them made any mistake at all, the other could die. Their lives, quite literally, depended on one another. They have no choice but to face decision-making, share ideas about what to do next, and to execute those choices, together. Simple acts, like making sure the other person has enough water or double-checking to make sure their equipment is secure, in the wrong context might seem like micromanaging or a lack of trust. But when it comes from a trusted

> **Really great partners know that being committed to the partnership means that your best day is a day in which your partner has her best day.**

partner with the right intention, instead it shows that someone really cares about who you are and that your safety and your well-being are essential to the success of the company.

As Collins explained, really great partners know that being committed to the partnership means that your best day is a day in which your partner has her best day. Since that lunch, I have done my best to internalize the intention to really care about my partners as if my own life depends on it.

What to Look for in a Partner

There are so many considerations when it comes to choosing a partner. The next few sections are intended to break down the primary tenets of what makes a good partnership, and how to identify certain red flags.

Considering how much risk-taking is involved in business, it's imperative that you find someone who you can trust with your money and your well-being. The process of making decisions, even though only one person has the ultimate authority, is the difference maker. Initially take a solid amount of time to discuss the vision, the core values, the mission of the business, and the exit plan. Through these conversations, you get to know each other. Spend time together in new and different situations. Learn how each handles stress and emotionally charged situations and how they recharge. Check references, both personal and professional. Finally, plan the long-term strategy before signing documents that bind you together.

Decision-Making

The larger the operations of the company, the more important it is to test that you are on the same page about the process of decision-making. What is the structure for decision-making? Who is part of the conversation, and who is excluded? Who frames the discussion?

Is it one person, majority rule, or consensus? Does everyone have an equal say in the vote, regardless of rank, investment, or experience? If not, how are these discussions weighted? If the vote isn't unanimous, who gets the deciding vote? Discuss your communication styles: How are you going to communicate? How often are you going to have meetings? Who is going to go to the meetings—just the partners, or everyone in the organization? Are you going to form an advisory board? If so, what kinds of skill sets do you want to bring to the table?

Have a hard conversation about money as well: How do you compensate yourself? How are you going to accelerate growth? What happens if you need to raise more money? What are the expectations for growth? Does everyone have the same goals for becoming a six, a fifteen, or a fifty-million-dollar company? Make sure you share your goals for the exit strategy: What happens if someone wants to leave the partnership? Does someone have to be bought out to leave? What happens if, despite having a great product and excellent service, no one wants to pay for it? What happens if you run out of money?

Let's face it, business is about the details. While the grand vision is full of exciting dreams and limitless possibility, the day-to-day involves small and specific details. It's one thing to determine that you are on the same page when it comes to your core values and missions, but it's quite another thing to find common ground on the minutiae.

How are you going to make business decisions with your suppliers, your vendors, your customers, and your marketing group? What are the obligations and expectations of each of these roles, and what are their functions? How do you delegate authority to get the work done?

How are you going to make sure that everyone stays in their lane and doesn't step on one another's toes? What happens when there are too many good choices and they all could be considered the right direction to go in? What happens if people within the company have disputes? Who mediates? What happens if mediation isn't effective?

It's imperative that these decisions are not just made but also documented—written down and formalized. From experience, I have found that outside advisors, both financial and legal, are extremely helpful in formalizing this kind of documentation. If you get these details committed to paper first, when everything is rosy and optimistic, when things get sticky, when things get tense (which they always will, eventually), you can return to the documentation instead of having to make decisions during a heated moment.

Find Someone with Whom You Can Share Anything

The most important thing in a partnership is making sure that you share core values. But it's not enough just to define these values together once, at the formation of the company. You must also keep them in the front of your mind and commit to holding one another accountable to the stated values. In my company, Flexability, we put people first, keep our promises, and lead with abundance, bravery, and courage. These are our core values. We use a simple annual system for rating one another, to make sure that each year we haven't taken a step back from our goal of living into our values. Our system includes a series of pluses and minuses to indicate where we feel that one has succeeded in our communal goals and where we need to invite the other to "lean in" if we are having an issue. Checking in yearly on whether our values need to be updated, always holding each other accountable, is key to our successful partnership. This is more than just a marketing strategy; it is a series of goals and values that you live into in the day-to-day operations of the company. Because, as best-selling author Gino Wickman talks about in his book *What the Heck is EOS?*, if you could tell a story about your core values, and really find a hundred people who leaned into and lived that core value, you could solve any issue, including world peace. You could solve clean water. You could solve world hunger. There isn't anything you couldn't do with a team that is as committed and as connected as that.

Check In with Your Partners Early and Often

These are the kinds of conversations to have frequently and at length with the leaders, stakeholders, and influencers in the company. Make sure that you are all, still, very much on the same page. Clear your calendar, cancel your meetings, and gather outside the office. Clear the whiteboard, and agree that nothing is out-of-bounds for discussion. What issues exist? Decide the priority? What's urgent and immediate? What's important and timely? What should we be doing differently? Where should we start? What's working? What's not working? On an annual basis, ask "If we were going to redo everything today, what would we change? What would we keep the same?" Do it without the threat of reprisal or judgment, and do your best to encourage honesty and openness. My partners and I often use the phrase "debate like you're right, and listen like you're wrong."

Surround Yourself with the Right People

Partnership is, in many ways, a series of concentric rings. In those outer circles are the people who perhaps you don't know as well or haven't worked with for as long a time. These relationships tend to be more general and more formal. But as you move in toward the center of the circle, partnerships become more specific and more intimate. Vulnerability becomes a necessity, and letting your guard down is a sign of trust. At the center of the circle are extraordinary conversations during which there is great risk and great reward.

It's at this central place, this fine pinpoint, where the extraordinary conversations take place. It is here that you can sit in the midst of your discomfort. There's no shame, no threat of reprisal. This is the place where "If you think it, say it," because you are in a place of complete and total trust with your partners. It's in this extraordinary conversation that innovation, creativity, and risk-taking bubble up. There's a feeling of abundance, as if there were no constraint on resources. It's a place of plenty and of wonder.

It's in these center relationships where partners who trust one another admit fault, show weakness, and challenge each other to do better in every way. You can invite one another to poke holes in each other's arguments and invite one another to think more deeply, making visible the gaps in logic. While in another circumstance, this may seem like aggressive or cruel behavior, in a truly trusting and connected partnership, this kind of work is truly an act of love. It is wanted and invited, and certainly not something I would invite just anyone to do.

Committing to a Partnership

A partnership requires a choice, a decision. "Do I want to enter into a transformational relationship with this person?" "Can I fully trust them to encourage me to be my highest and best self and to challenge me and hold me accountable when I'm not?" When two or more parties agree to cooperate, in the name of advancing their mutual interest, it truly is a gift. It's about being seen and being heard. And when that complete trust is there, even if there is an inkling of a doubt about a project or an idea, there is the ability to say "Let's do it" anyway, because there is so much faith in that person and that partnership. The best partnerships can be both deep and long term because of that commitment that is made, which can withstand the challenges in the road, the failings, and the stress of success as well.

Being in a Partnership

Like Jim Collins says, "my best day is when my partner has a great day." The best way to invite psychological safety into a partnership is to approach the relationship with a mindset of abundance, where there is always enough and little constraint on resources. Each person will do what it takes to make sure that each partner feels that they belong, that they are included and valued for their unique contributions.

This means that I'm constantly thinking about my partners, I'm asking questions and staying curious. Rather than making assumptions about what is going on in their head, I ask. We communicate early and often. I listen with my eyes as well as my ears, paying attention to not just what is being said but what is behind the words as well. What is the story they are telling? Where does it come from? What emotions does it provoke? If your partner doesn't feel that psychological safety and inclusion, then they aren't going to be able to deeply connect. If you can't achieve a deep connection, that lack of connection is ultimately going to challenge growth in the relationship and growth in the business.

There is a quote from leadership expert Brené Brown that I like to share with my clients. It's from a speech she gave at the South by Southwest festival in 2016. She explains, "We like to think we are rational beings who occasionally have an emotion and flick it away and carry on being rational." But in truth, she clarified, "We are emotional, feeling beings, who, on rare occasions, think." I love this quote because it rings so true for me. We can talk all day about our business plans and strategies, our work structures and organizational models, and we are absolutely dominated by our emotions. Often we forget that there is a difference between reaction and response to stimuli. As leaders and partners, we must hold space for the reaction and accept the consequences when all those emotions go haywire. I have found that my most successful partnerships are the ones that are galvanized by an abundance mindset. We show appreciation for challenging one another and encouraging each other to speak truth and share our visions.

Conflict in Partnership

Conflict in partnerships is absolutely necessary. In fact, healthy, vigorous debate, disagreement, and conflict are to be welcomed. Some of my greatest opportunities and achievements were born from chaos and disruption of the status quo.

While teaching science fiction literature to high school students, I asked the students to "suspend disbelief." When you suspend your disbelief, you stop thinking in terms of rules and constraints. Just for a moment, everything is possible. I have found that this phrase is equally as useful when describing conflict in business as it is for describing alternative worlds on other planets. This suspension of

When you suspend your disbelief, you stop thinking in terms of rules and constraints.

disbelief is a necessary mindset for approaching healthy conflict. In a vigorous debate, you need to listen with intention, and you must hear every idea. Every idea is interesting or clever. Invite your colleagues to walk down a path of seeming impossibility with you. And if you are invited to suspend your disbelief and hear out an idea from your partner that sounds too risky or unfamiliar, listen with an open heart and open mind. Listen as if your beliefs are uninformed. Hold your colleagues, far-fetched ideas and all, in faith and confidence.

If you can get past the initial discomfort, really go down deep to that place of openness and vulnerability, there is a place of agreement— if not complete agreement, then at least a place of understanding and acknowledgment and gratitude for one another. This level of trust is important for the creativity and transformation that is necessary to keep building and scaling up your business.

In Good Times and Bad

Often, at the beginning of any business venture, there is a period when the business is just getting off the ground and it's not yet financially viable. The early stages of the business, especially one that is self-funded, is where partners may experience the most tension and disagreement about every detail. That's why it's so important to make sure that you and your partners have talked through the different scenarios that consider the risk and reward of running a business. Ask your potential partner, right off the bat, "What's your relationship to money?" "What is your risk tolerance?" "Could you go a year without making any money?" I have learned from experience that asking these questions and discussing various outcomes saves future conflict and aids the growth planning process. Very few businesses are going to attract "big" money early and achieve a 5X or 10X valuation. Most businesses, on the other hand, follow a predictable model which starts with an initial cash infusion that is spent on people and activities that everyone hopes will generate revenue to stay in business long enough to generate a profit.

After leaving the law firm, I formed an exploratory advisory group to support the growth of women-led businesses. For the nine months before we legally formed the company, we talked strategy going on retreats, playing cards and watching sports together. We built camaraderie and trust. Unfortunately, for all the work we had put into our project, we couldn't quite figure out how to monetize it. I would say we were about ten years ahead of our time, because now, similar consultancies are doing business and serving this need. We ultimately disbanded before our service made it out of beta testing. We did all the "right" planning activities with the right people, but the marketplace was not ready to buy what we had to sell.

Plan Your Exit Strategy

There's bound to be challenges, changes, and transformation, and sometimes partnerships can weather that storm, and sometimes they can't. But even the greatest of partnerships must come to an end. Sometimes this means a change in the partnership agreement, and sometimes it means a formal exit. Exits come in many forms: selling to a competitor or a customer, selling out to one or more partners, selling to do something new, selling to retire, or selling to get out. Regardless, it is a breakup of a relationship.

If you're lucky, this breakup will be amicable, full of love and mutual respect. Hopefully, you can hear and see your partner and their wants and needs, and bear no judgment for their choice or for your own. However, things don't always work out that way. That's why it's so important to plan your exit strategy at the beginning and document the process in the company operating agreements. Although it seems counterintuitive, it's much better to plan these things well in advance when everything is rosy and everyone is getting along so it doesn't become a knock-down, drag-out emotionally dramatic and draining situation. Although a partnership can feel like a band of brothers or a tight knit community, it's imperative that the documentation is there for when things go wrong.

Other Kinds of Business Partnerships

We've talked specifically about partners and partnerships within a company, but there are other kinds of partnerships outside of your team members that are critical to business growth and crucial to the experience of feeling connected in the work you do. I'm going to spend a little bit of time discussing those partnerships here.

Client Partnerships

Clients also have the potential to be partners, especially clients who share your core values as well as an alignment of purpose. These ideal clients don't come along every day, but when they do, hang on to them. At any given time, we at Flexability only have a handful of this type of client, but when they call me up and say "We need you," I can tell you, I am on the very next flight out to go visit them. I would go to the ends of the earth for them.

Once you get comfortable and established in your business and the services that you provide, you will have the opportunity to pick and choose your clients. You will have the luxury to turn down those potential clients that don't share your values and those clients who will be more trouble than they are worth. How many of us have had clients where the effort it would take to please them simply wasn't worth the compensation? It's always an amazing feeling to find a client who shares the same desire to bend the universe with you—a company that wants to change the world, not by breaking it but just by bending it a little bit, to make it a little bit more inclusive with empathy, gratitude, and appreciation. Those are the kinds of clients who I want to support and who want to support me.

Suppliers as Partners

Although it is not common for people to think of their suppliers as their partners, in truth, these are some of your most valuable relationships. Your suppliers are those from whom you buy services and products. When you connect with, and make a purchase from, a supplier, you can buy from someone who aligns with your values. They have a stakeholder mentality in your business rather than a shareholder mentality. This means that they care about the well-being of your company, even if they don't have a financial investment. If you do well, they do well. You are, after all, their client. And a good relationship with a supplier can mean smooth, predictable, and fair transactions for years to come. Mistakes are easily addressed when this relationship is built on integrity and trust. These partners work together and help each other with the goal of mutual success.

At Flexability, we teach and train around equity and inclusion, with a focus on helping companies improve their culture with a long-term goal of building high-performance teams. To live into our values of inclusion in a broader sense, we do our best to buy from companies who also put their values of affecting change at the forefront of their mission and culture. We want to support them so that they can continue to grow and do their good work, just as we want to grow and do valuable work. We consider this each time we decide where we spend our dollars. For example, our marketing agency is a women-owned South African communications firm that is most notable for their work with the Nelson Mandela Foundation. Although the time difference can be a challenge, I think it's wonderful to work with a company that is making a difference in their community and their nation.

Spend your dollars in line with your values. Buy local, and support independent businesses and artists. It keeps the money in the neighborhood and supports local artists and businesses. Across the United States, small businesses employ more of the workforce than all the Fortune 500 companies put together. According to the US Small Business Administration Office of Advocacy, small businesses have generated 64 percent of the new jobs over the past fifteen years.[23] Small businesses are the backbone of our economy, nationally and globally.

Peer Groups

A peer learning group is also important to your growth as an industry leader. These are organizations that bring together people in similar roles, often joined by another commonality such as an industry or an identity. An example is the organization that I referred to earlier: the Women Presidents Organization that brought together women CEOs for networking, learning, and camaraderie.

Now, despite some commonly held beliefs, this kind of organization isn't a fraternity or a sorority. These more formalized networks,

23   Phil Cohen, "Small Business or Big Business: Which Really Creates the Most Jobs?" Find Factors, August 8, 2022, https://www.factorfinders.com/small-business-job-creation-vs-big.

ideally, will lead to individual relationships that can exist outside of the conferences and group activities. The goal is really to find a handful of people who understand your unique situation and challenge you to be your best. What you are paying for when you join one of these organizations is for someone to facilitate peer learning. You are paying for a formally trained facilitator to guide you through the process of framing and discussing common problems.

We act as an informal board of advisors who challenge each other to think differently. We also discuss problems that more often affect women in the workplace, such as pay equity, health and wellness, access to capital, and getting board of directors appointments. We can call or message one another, day or night, to talk through both business and personal challenges.

Networking Groups

However, before joining any group, be sure you know what your intentions are, and be very clear about it. A recent article in the *Harvard Business Review* posits that most networking events aren't worth the free drink ticket you get upon entry.[24] This can be even more the case for an introvert like me, who finds these kinds of social occasions to be quite draining. But while I have had my fair share of wasted afternoons at networking events, I have also found that they can be extremely useful if you go in with a very clear plan. If you know your purpose, on a deeper level than just "networking," these can be rare opportunities to connect with senior people you might not otherwise be able to access. Before committing to attend, ask yourself "Why this event?" "Who do I want to meet?" "What's my goal of meeting this

---

24   Derek Coburn, "Don't Waste Your Time on Networking Events," *Harvard Business Review*, September 26, 2016, https://hbr.org/2016/09/dont-waste-your-time-on-networking-events.

person?" "Is there someone there who can facilitate an introduction?" And perhaps most importantly: "What's my plan to follow up?"

Advisors and Sponsors as Partners

It's all too easy for a business leader, especially an entrepreneur, to act as though they can handle everything on their own. Though it may feel as though we are inventing a new way of doing business, the truth is many people have experienced similar ups and downs of running a business. There is no reason to reinvent the wheel. When the universe comes to you and says "Here is an advisor, a mentor, or a sponsor," pay attention. Someone with expertise and different experience will know how to help you with strategy, and hopefully they will be able to connect you with new clients, new employees, new money, and new services.

I have a professor from business school who has offered to act as an advisor to me. Whenever I need her help, she's ready, willing, and able to offer her advice. She has helped me get over those rough patches in my professional life, because she sees me in a way that no one else does. I repeat certain phrases that she said to me years ago that instantly come to the surface and are suddenly applicable. I am so grateful for this relationship and the conversations we have shared.

When you find those people who can offer you these kinds of relationships, know that it is a true gift. From an abundance mindset, the best thing you can do is to humble yourself to receive what's being offered. Because even if you are a great leader, there is always, always room for growth and improvement. Let people help you grow, expand your repertoire, and guide you to becoming your best self.

The Takeaways

1. Know your core values, and tell stories about each one.

2. Choose courage over comfort, and speak the truth.

3. Write out all the details from beginning to end, including exit strategies at various company milestones.

4. Build a network of peer advisors who are emotionally invested in your success as a leader.

5. Be prepared to let go to protect your well-being.

CHAPTER 7

A Purposeful Implementation

Listen with attention and intention. As Yoda puts it so adeptly to Luke, 'Do or do not. There is no try.'
—NANCY GEENEN

There comes a moment in many leaders' careers where they reach a tipping point that requires an intentional decision: Dig deeper and do the work, or continue to tread lightly and perhaps forgo the dream? In making this decision, the choice is between settling for what's "good enough" and choosing to work toward mastery. There's nothing inherently wrong with good enough. Good enough, is after all, still good. The leap from good to great doesn't necessarily need a massive reordering of every known thing. Because we are so attached to, and comfortable in, the status quo, even a small leap may take a massive amount of bravery and then consistent effort.

Like so many instances of growth, this moment often happens at a point of suffering, emotional and/or financial. We've all been there: the burnout, the drain, the feeling of not being enough in a work/life dance that is skewed toward work. It's at this moment that we know that something must give, and someone must change. When you are able to fully acknowledge to yourself that the things you've been doing do not give you joy, that's your tipping point. Ignoring the lack of joy is not an option. Choosing change is scary, and it is the way to move forward.

My Personal Tipping Point

I was in my forties and working at the law firm in San Francisco. I had been promoted to office managing partner of the Northern California offices and had been doing that job consistently for the past seven years. Our leadership team achieved a remarkable financial turnaround; we changed the culture and grew the headcount threefold over my tenure as managing partner. We acquired a new practice group in a new geography. The administrative team ran the day-to-day operations, freeing up the lawyers to focus on their work. While I loved leading a team and trying cases, I didn't love, and admittedly was not particularly good at, managing my peers.

It was in this moment, in this frame of mind, that I flew to headquarters for the annual compensation presentation for the partners in the offices that I led. The CEO and firm managing partner asked me for a premeeting the day before my presentation. I was sitting face-to-face across from the CEO, and he very calmly informed me that he was going to replace me as the office managing partner. I was devastated. I had walked in expecting a giant "atta girl." I didn't know what to do or what to say. I just sat there, dumbfounded. Of course, we had a conversation about the rationale and new direction. I do not remember one word of the why. I dutifully gave input to the candidates under consideration to succeed me. I showed up the next day and presented my compensation package recommendations to the executive committee. A close colleague explained that I had lost touch with the partners in my office while I was focused on my own career. I countered defensively: of course, I had been in three different jury trials over the last eighteen months. What mattered was my relationships with my partners in the office were suffering, and those partners complained. I moved my office in Palo Alto. I stayed on at the firm for another two years. Team members continued to seek out my advice and guidance. I realized I was no longer a good "fit" for the firm culture.

Upon reflection, and although I will never be able to say for sure, I have a hunch that my coming out as a lesbian may have scared the firm leadership. I had been asked to come out, officially, as part of a more public push for visibility in diversity among the firm. Most of the management committee were older straight white men who may not have been ready for "other." I never asked. I did not speak up, nor did I ask questions. There were only a few women and one person of color at the table. An LGBTQ+ member may have been a step too far.

Changing Paths

For me, tipping point moments remind me of the Robert Frost poem "The Road Not Taken," in which he writes

> Two roads diverged in a wood, and I—
> I took the one less traveled by,
> And that has made all the difference.

I found myself at a crossroads. I had always been a lawyer, and I very much could have continued practicing law in the same, or even a new, environment. It would have been the "good enough" path to take. I felt compelled to go in a different direction, try something new. I shifted my mindset about the meaning of work, personal and professional relationships. I found myself in a moment where I recognized that I could choose. In essence, a career crisis spelled opportunity. It became my "bend the universe" moment. I had all the tools I needed to take a step in that next direction.

It wasn't all at once, of course; these kinds of decisions rarely are. Often it felt like I wasn't just taking the path "less taken" but the path that barely existed at all. I was hacking my way through the jungle thicket with a dull machete. Every low point truly is an opportunity for growth and change. I decided that I would get back up, even after getting knocked down too many times in a row.

Finding My Community

I had been lucky enough to have stumbled into a peer network several years prior, which was my saving grace and my anchor in this storm. Early in my days as office managing partner, I learned that a group of women used our conference room one Monday night a month. Curious to know who these women were, I found out that they were a peer-networking group called the Women Presidents Organization (WPO). It seemed to me that if we were letting them use our space and providing them with food and drinks, I should, at the very least, go and pitch our law firm's services to them. After spending a couple of dinners with them, I quickly realized that this was an organization that I very much wanted to join. The entire gamut of women leaders was represented. Some of these women were running businesses that were still in the hobby stage, some ran lifestyle businesses providing financial security and a career path for their families, and others were at the helm of large privately owned companies. If, as Madeleine Albright said, "There's a special place in hell for women who don't help women," then this conference room, once a month, was heaven. Each of these women were committed to helping and caring for one another.

Every woman in the group had a story about getting knocked down and getting back up again and learning throughout the process. I listened to their stories of resilience, saw how they turned challenges into opportunities. Each of these women shared their tipping point moments. They showed interest in each other's passion and shared their strengths and skills while also revealing vulnerabilities in their lives and their businesses. I learned my experience as a woman leader was not unique. Failure was not conquering the feelings of shame and blame. Success is learning from the missteps, mistakes, and errors in judgment. This group exemplified the mattering and belonging that I craved. And they connected me with subject matter experts who helped me focus on my presence, my communication skills, and my emotional intelligence. I disclosed my deepest fears and discovered that I was lovable. These women supported me through my transition to entrepreneurship. I learned that I loved the process of running a business as much as I loved trying a case to a jury.

I could hear my mother's voice in my head saying "If you don't think you're good, no one else will either." I knew I had to believe in myself. I knew I had to dust myself off and focus on two things: What was I passionate about, and what did I do well? I took time to really consider what value I could bring to a company and what opportunities I already had right in front of me.

I loved the world of business too much to ever leave it. I knew business. I turned an unprofitable office to profitable. Under my management, the office doubled in size. I opened and closed offices. I hired a professional management team. We trained new attorneys and other legal professionals. We created a mission and vision with a culture of inclusiveness. I learned about the Entrepreneurial Operating System (EOS), a set of concepts and practical tools that help entrepreneurs launch and run their companies. I made my declaration as an entrepreneur to the WPO chapter members and prepared to start my first business.

Entering Back into the Business World

I launched a consulting company for women. It was completely focused on how women-owned businesses grow. The attempt was to gather all the skills and experience of the lawyers, accountants, economists and marketers, salespeople, and legal experts that we had in our Women Presidents Organization and turn it into a profitable service-oriented business. Although the company didn't get past the early pilot contracts, I do have something I'm quite proud of to show for that time. When I was recruiting for a woman finance advisor, I met the person who would become my wife. I'm happy to report that our relationship has had more lasting power than that first business!

As I was transitioning to the next entrepreneurial endeavor, I earned a scholarship from the Women Presidents Organization to Harvard Business School's Owner/President Management (OPM) program. For three years in a row, over 150 entrepreneurs spent three weeks at Harvard Business School learning from Harvard's top professors in the Business School. In fact, one the professors that I met at the Harvard Business School is a dear friend and serves as a tireless advisor and consultant for my current company.

Prior to starting at Harvard, I built the next business. I took a step back and took a good hard look at my interests and skills and realized that I was still quite interested in trying cases. I still had many connections to law firms, senior trial attorneys, and litigators. I had always enjoyed law and wanted to build a company that focused on trial consulting. Like the first company, this project was entirely self-funded and utilized EOS to get off the ground. But unlike the first project, this company was 100 percent focused on where we were going and how we were going to get there. In less than five years, we had built up our company from just a way to pay the bills to a six-million-dollar company.

While I was proud of the work we were doing with the company, I must admit we weren't able to find the partners I felt that we needed to scale the company to ten million. I sold my equity to my cofounder, who still leads this successful company. Although I made sure that all our loans were paid off with interest, I admit, it still wasn't the easiest process. A business is really like a marriage, and the breakup of a business relationship feels like a divorce.

> # A business is really like a marriage, and the breakup of a business relationship feels like a divorce.

It's messy, it's upsetting, and it's emotionally draining. Ultimately, in the end, I knew it was the right decision for me. I then did what I think every good leader should do when they are burned out and don't quite know what to do with themselves next. I took some time off! I really wanted to take some time to think about what was next before I dived headlong into the next project.

I sat on several boards and prioritized volunteering my time. I was financially secure at that time, owing to my healthy relationship to money. I focused on learning parenting, a gift I thought I would not experience. I coached at the local high school. I trusted the universe and my WPO posse, who advised me to enjoy the family time. I also knew that I would step back into the workforce at the right time, whether as the interim CEO of a company or as a UPS driver!

The Workforce Summons

During this second hiatus, I continued my service as the vice chair of the board of directors of the temporary staffing firm for individuals with disabilities. I continued my relationship with the WPO as the facilitator of the local Silicon Valley chapter that involved monthly meetings as well as extensive facilitation training. I found that, much like my love of coaching high school softball, I really loved coaching business leaders as well. I found I was quite good at drawing people out of their shells. Having come out the other side of this journey, I knew how to gently encourage others to do so as well.

It was right around this time that the board chair of the staffing company asked me to step in as the interim CEO. While I had already been the CEO of two successful companies, I was now tasked with stepping into the role of leading something I hadn't founded. As a self-funding nonprofit, the organization had the potential to grow tenfold as a tech company that employed individuals with disabilities. The business required a complete overhaul, because it had yet to go digital. We were a $20 million business with a healthy reserve for investment in growth. I worked as interim CEO for this for two years. We built a professional management team and focused the organization mindset on sustainable growth. We created a culture of stakeholder primacy, putting people first. At the end of two years, the board felt ready to hire a full-time CEO. As a true visionary, I was ready for the next challenge.

I could feel myself being pulled in two different directions. On one hand, I really loved leading a company and building high-performing teams. I had to learn to get out of the way. I had spent years studying the humanity of leadership, and by this point I really felt I had the skills to reach into somebody's heart and quickly figure out what made it tick. On the other hand, I was a total geek for the structures and processes on which great companies run. I loved using EOS[25] in my companies because the leadership team aligned with the goals and mission of the company. As an entrepreneur, I had seen it used successfully countless times.

I decided to go to EOS boot camp. I wanted to become an implementer of that system and to learn it inside and out. While this decision may seem to be purely business minded, it was quite a personal decision. If there is one thing I can't stress enough to other entrepreneurs, it's to find an operating system that works for you. There are a whole host of them, and while my personal favorite is EOS, there are several other well-regarded systems. Find the one that aligns with your heart and your business acumen, and lean into the discipline and accountability that are offered to you. And of course, be mindful of the time it will take to get the rest of your team on board with the program as well. It won't be a fast change. When the work is done, you will all be a part of the same train, with all the cars linked up and ready to charge ahead. A familiar EOS value: Go slow to go fast.

25　Entrepreneurial Operating System, based on the book *Traction*, by Gino Wickman.

Flexability Begins

I wish I knew then what I know now. Each decision has brought me one step closer to doing what I love and that at which I excel. When it finally crystalized in my mind, it was as if the idea had been there the whole time, just waiting for the right moment to emerge. I care about equity at work. I care about vulnerability and accountability in the workplace. I also care about systems, structures, and operating systems. I love being a coach and a teacher of those individuals committed to do the work toward mastery.

I shared my vision of equity and inclusion as part of the overall business strategy. After the internal announcement of my exit from the recruiting firm, the leadership team celebrated our successes and discussed what was next. I'll never forget that moment when our VP of sales looked right at me and said "Nancy, we've got to do this with a broader equity lens. When it comes to ideas about diversity, equity, and inclusion, you are already doing it. You may not know the right words, but your ideas are already there. We should really do it for real." Well, that was all the push I needed. It had taken me years of experience, networking and connecting with others, to gather my team together to have exactly the right people in the room with me for this big idea. But at last, here we were—my group of kindred spirits who wanted to "bend the universe" with me. We all knew we wanted to have an impact, and we knew we wanted to help other companies create equity in their workplace. But it was still a little unclear what our focus was. Were we going to focus on disabilities? Were we going to focus on race? What about LGBTQ+ issues? But in the end, we decided that we didn't want to parse it out like that. We really wanted to create a company that prioritized and uplifted all those identities. Had I not gone through the ups and downs of the past five years, I don't think I would have figured out that I didn't need to pick a single issue. We could approach equity and inclusion from a holistic and stakeholder perspective. The people I had gathered with me loved the idea. Of the people who were in the room with me at the time, three are principals with the company today.

Our energy and commitment were well timed, poised, and ready to meet the moment. For a start-up, 2020 was a grueling year in so many respects. No one anticipated the dramatic effects COVID-19 would have on our lives. The social movements #MeToo and Black Lives Matter, the anniversary of the Americans with Disabilities Act, the Dakota Access Pipeline protests at Standing Rock, and Juneteenth celebrations brought to light the absolute pressing need to address issues of gender and racial justice, not just in our communities but everywhere from the stockroom to the boardroom.

The work of equity and inclusion became the focus of our organization. We were finding our way as a new business using EOS with an equity and inclusion lens. I led as a visionary. Our integrator inspired us to plan the work and work the plan. We grew, we contracted, and we found our sweet spot. We had the right people in the room.

The Future of Equity and Inclusion in the Workplace

I am hopeful that the acceptance that we have fought so hard for— ideas of mattering and belonging, of curiosity and care, being seen and heard—will soon be givens. The new generations in the workspace care deeply about company culture, demonstrated by the diversity of identities at all levels of leadership. The younger principals in my company intrinsically understand and live these values effortlessly. I am grateful for the opportunity to live and learn with my colleagues. I am grateful that I decided that "good enough" was just not for me.

When we started Flexability as a social impact firm, we set our core values of people first, integrity to do what you say, and a growth mindset. I wanted that laser focus on our culture of stakeholder primacy. We began by focusing on management, creating different expectations around how a manager "shows up." We built it from the ground up, thinking through communication, asking questions, and receiving information. We wanted management to be fluid and built into the system. As Jim Collins says, "The moment you feel the need to tightly manage someone, you've made a hiring mistake. The best people don't need to be managed. Guided, taught, led … yes. But not tightly managed." We wanted to help our clients find the right people to hire, as well as how to manage them in a way that everyone felt they belonged and mattered. For Gen Xers and millennials, there is nothing confusing or contradictory about vulnerability and accountability in the workplace. It makes perfect sense to them. In their minds, it would be absurd to expect one leader to have all the answers. They know that leadership isn't so much about perfection as it's about trusting your team and knowing how to hold them accountable for their actions and their behaviors.

We wanted to make sure that we were building a system that created opportunities for everyone, based on their passions, strengths, and interests. If a teammate's passions and strengths don't match up with the job they've been hired to do, it's like trying to grow a fern in the desert. It certainly is doable, but it's going to take a lot of time, effort, and resources that should be devoted to others. Instead, we

> I am grateful that I decided that "good enough" was just not for me.

wanted to help clients grow the right plants in the best environment for growth. Learn people's interests and strengths and find the right place in the company for them to flourish. Each company really is a unique ecosystem. Everything must align, and all the pieces have to fit together. Whether we are talking about profits, partners, or people, having equity and inclusion as an integral part of that purposeful implementation works best when it's built into the foundation of the entire operating system.

With equity and inclusion already a part of the system, there is often still the need for creating diversity. This work must be about more than tokenism. One is never enough. We must advocate for the rule of three: In a 2016 interview, Icelandic woman leaders discussed "the rule of three" as a key to the advances women have made toward equality there. In their experience, one woman on a board or in an organization will not have enough support for her ideas. Even two women will not have much influence. But once you get three or more women in a group, the culture of the group changes.[26]

Improvement in diversity metrics is a result of systemic equity and inclusion processes in every function of a company. Choosing a benchmark, increasing the diversity of your staff by 25 percent each year, requires a commitment to a strategy supported by sufficient resources. Accountability and execution require that company leaders examine all processes to root out bias. I'm advocating for slow and steady progress that celebrates achievement of declared goals along the way. People leaders must get sufficient resources of time, people, and capital to effect change over a period of time.

But metrics aren't enough to build a great culture. First, leaders must get comfortable with "otherness" and self-identification. Gay,

---

26 Gretchen Jennings, "The Rule of Three," Museum Commons, May 25, 2016, https://museumcommons.com/2016/05/the-rule-of-three.html.

disabled, neurodiverse—these are sample labels that we as leaders must embrace. Socializing the commitment to equity in the workplace requires that all leaders are engaged in the mission. Early on there may be a tension between outside hires to increase diversity metrics and current team members on a leadership trajectory. This tension is a choice between "two rights." particularly for a senior leadership team. Every company is unique and must still make a choice. Creating that culture of inclusivity in your firm, in your working groups, in your day-to-day activities, is the elixir for developing diverse, high-performing teams.

So, before you begin this journey toward diversity, equity, and inclusion, really take some time to ask yourself "What do I stand for? What work have I already done? What work remains? Book clubs, podcasts, and lectures are a great start! How am I stepping outside of my comfort zone to do the hard work, both on myself as well as within my company?"

Figure out what you stand for, and then take a stand.

The Takeaways

1. Choose courage over comfort.

2. Choose accountability over shame and blame.

3. Choose a peer network that challenges your status quo.

4. Choose joy over suffering.

5. Choose abundance over scarcity.

CONCLUSION

Pay attention to the verbs.
—MARCUS BUCKINGHAM, *NEW YORK TIMES* BEST-SELLING
AUTHOR AND FOUNDER OF STRENGTHS REVOLUTION

As we come to the end of this book, I want to encourage you to take some time to look at the way that you frame the world around you. You may not realize it, but the way you see things and the way you approach the world is evident in everything you do, particularly the way you speak.

We all know a person who, no matter what the circumstances, always frames the world around them by the things that were done to them, not the things that they caused to happen. They say things like "The traffic made me late" instead of the acknowledgment that "I was late because I didn't account for the traffic." While it may seem to garner empathy from other people when one frames their tardiness on something that was beyond their control, the reality is it removes all agency from the circumstance. Acknowledging your own contribution to the event reframes you as an agent in your life. You have the power to choose. You are an active participant in your life and not merely a helpless bystander.

Don't try when it comes to equity and inclusion. Just do. Doing is a process. It doesn't happen overnight, and it doesn't have to be done exactly right from the outset, but if you are only committing to trying, you haven't really decided to *do*. Doing requires intention, attention, and action. Start small; schedule time on your calendar every day to do one thing that improves the feeling of mattering and belonging for your team.

When you commit to doing, you are making a commitment to working on yourself. When you decide to do, instead of just try, you are taking on a leadership role for the rest of the group. Make a commitment, here and now, to doing.

Study Yourself

In a keynote speech by Marcus Buckingham to the Women Presidents Organization, he asked his audience, "When was the last time you spent any time studying yourself?" In this room full of women leaders and women CEOs, you could have heard a pin drop. You as a business leader are not separate from you as a human being. You as a business leader are also not separate from the company itself. Leaders don't deliver the message; they are the message.

Growth is hard, and if there is one thing that I work on every day, it's recognizing my own discomfort. When I feel pushback, when that creeping feeling of "I don't want to" comes into my mind, I ask myself "What is this resistance about?" "What happens if I work to overcome it?" I sit in the midst of my discomfort and work on the origin of the emotion. I practice choosing courage over comfort, which means I don't let negative emotions, fear, shame, scarcity, hold me back. I recognize the emotion and then push through, sometimes just because I want to see if I can do so.

Find What You Love

Dan Sullivan, founder and president of Strategic Coach, has made it a practice of asking "What is your unique ability?" I have learned from many of the business leaders and workplace luminaries that I follow that great leadership begins with wanting to work hard at developing that unique ability. Ask yourself, "What is the thing that I love doing, and that I'm really good at, and that, when I do it, the time just flies by?" A truly great leader is a person who can do that, not just for themselves but also for the team as well. If there are parts of the job in which you don't find joy, don't work against your natural tendencies. Your goal should be to find that exact right person who will thank their lucky stars to do the thing you like least for which they have the skills to do well.

Curiosity Leads to Knowledge

A characteristic of true leadership is childlike curiosity and the willingness to be a beginner. It's that growth mindset that knows that one is never truly done learning. A curious child doesn't look at people who are different from them with judgment, embarrassment, or revulsion. They simply approach the world with wonder and curiosity. They want to know *why* a person in a wheelchair

A characteristic of true leadership is childlike curiosity and the willingness to be a beginner.

must navigate the world like that, but there is nothing cruel in their curiosity. The child likes learning new things and is unencumbered by "what success looks like."

The experience of writing this book has given me a new perspective, and I can say in complete sincerity that it has been humbling to realize there are still so many things I have to learn on my path toward mastery. Unlike a few decades ago, when I was so busy trying to "fake it 'til I make it" and "get it all right," I have learned now that it's much more important to settle into the process with patience, curiosity, and humility. I want to get better and have committed to new activities that will help me do so. It's my hope that everyone who reads this book, or even just flips through the pages, can get the message to do the self-work to become self-aware. You've got to continue to do the work, staying true to yourself and your strengths every step of the way but also staying aware of where the path to mastery may take you.

Keep Learning

Bettering yourself doesn't come from the simple desire to do so. Take small, intentional, and actionable steps every day. Putting in a bit of work each day results in small improvements. It may not seem like much until you look back at the progress you have made. The cumulative effect of small efforts results in big changes.

I made the commitment to read for at least two hours every day. Whether it's the news, fiction, nonfiction, essays, or research articles (I admit, I read a lot of research articles!), I decided that it's important to stay connected to the ever-changing ideas of the wider world, and reading is my preferred mode of learning. There are so many great thought leaders out there, including the handful I've mentioned in this book, such as Simon Sinek, Marcus Buckingham, Jim Collins,

Dan Sullivan, and Brené Brown. Find a thought leader that challenges and inspires and stick with them.[27]

Alternatively, if reading isn't your thing, you might find that podcasts, YouTube videos, documentary films, or even a thoughtful conversation with a friend works better for you. Just make sure that the information that you are consuming is asking you to think about new ideas and information and not necessarily telling you *what* to think about those ideas and information. Avoid the echo chamber, and sit in the midst of your discomfort. Do the work of thinking for yourself. It will strengthen your ability for critical analysis and decision-making.

Equity and Inclusion Begins with Trust

Early in my career, I realized I was a good coach and teacher. I also wanted to become an exceptional leader. To do so, I had to facilitate my own growth to grow a cohesive team through an equity and inclusion lens. I am not a natural container of safety, love, and heartfelt care. Over time, I learned that the way to do this is to begin with trust, as it's those high-trusting teams that are the ones that have the confidence to take risks without fear of threat or judgment. It's also that same team that can collectively develop an eye toward expanding the reach and the impact of the vision and mission of the company.

It is hard to challenge the status quo when our culture of twentieth-century "politeness" often tells us that it's bad manners to discuss race, gender, disability, or religion. Not talking about these workplace issues doesn't make them disappear. There have been major strides made in the twenty-first century. Conversations around race, gender identity, religion, and disability are becoming more and more

---

27   I have included my recommended reading list in the appendix.

common and carry less stigma. But there is still more work to do and particularly more work to be done in the workplace, where the culture of politeness over truth and accountability seems to be even more pervasive. But as business leaders, we don't want the workplace to be left behind in these very important conversations. Building a team that trusts each other enough to argue and to make space for one another to share is a key component of a high-performing team. Being able to debate and listen—in a healthy, loving way—and respectful is ultimately what creates that sense of trust and belonging.

As we create a culture of trust and accountability, our teams will choose courage over comfort. As the trust container fills up, teams believe they matter to the success of the organization. As we exemplify accountability over shame and blame, our teams start on the path of high performance. When the team trusts leadership and each other, they experience greatness. When leaders are willing to build a diverse team, business performance improves. The kaleidoscope of identities in the leadership team and throughout the organization is the competitive advantage.

You and Your Team Can Go Far

Working together means the team shares the trials and tribulations of the organization. The team experiences the big challenges that are both professionally and personally emotional. Relying on each other, a team can withstand pressure that one person could not shoulder alone. The team that trusts one another, engages in vigorous debate, commits to a shared goal with personal accountability gets results.[28] The leader is responsible for holding that safety container, that bucket

---

28   See *The Five Dysfunctions of a Team*, by Patrick Lencioni.

of trust, so that every team member feels safe and included as they venture forward toward greatness.

The workplace is a place where, over time, either the fear of rejection or the feeling of acceptance will come to dominate. People will either move through that space from a place of fear—I'm going to be judged, I'm under threat, I can't express myself—or they are going to come from a place of love—my thoughts and feelings are valued and matter, even if not everyone agrees with my analysis or recommendation.

All In

There is a greatness in a workspace where teammates press one another on the hard issues, challenging the assumptions and staying curious about the reasoning. Many times, the leader takes a step back and facilitates those conversations, pushing people to think deeper and harder about why they think the way that they do, to ask the questions that feel uncomfortable in the formation, and to listen as if hearing the idea for the first time. It's the difference between the usual conversation that is low risk and requires minimal energy and extraordinary high-risk, intentional debate where everyone on the team participates. Great leaders hold that space and facilitate those conversations in a way that makes all the participants feel seen and heard. It truly is an acquired skill that takes years of practice and requires vulnerability. The team leaves these meetings knowing that everyone has acted for the good of the company. All the input is well considered by all team members, and all participants have contributed by both listening and speaking. In the end, people may not always agree with one another or agree with the ultimate decision that gets made collectively, but everyone will know that they had the opportunity to listen and contribute and to debate with intention and curiosity, so that even if they don't like the direction the group decides to go in, they will be able to accept it.

These collective creative processes are the source of greatness. Building a great team should be the goal of every leader: a team where every member knows that they matter and belong. This is the place where the depth of the conversation is extraordinary and where great things happen, together.

The Big Takeaways

1. **Find a mentor and a coach.** Find someone who can support and guide you on your personal and professional journey. Find one or more persons who will assess and assist you with impartiality and honesty.

2. **Join a peer network.** A network that offers continuing education such as equity and inclusion, financial, and leadership education is ideal. This is particularly helpful if you are a woman, an LGBTQ+ person, or a BIPOC leader, who may experience things in the workplace that others don't see or lack familiarity.

3. **Form an advisory board.** When you have at least five full-time employees or you've crossed the $3 million mark in revenue, you are going to need a group of subject matter experts who will help you with strategy and growth. At $12 million, form a formal board of directors that understands your mission and vision and shares your core values.

4. **Continue your education.** Whether it's getting your GED, continuing your college education, taking executive education courses at a business school, or informally learning through reading, podcasts, and documentaries, make sure you are always learning and always advancing your knowledge.

5. **Stay in touch.** Stay connected to the most current issues and ideas by reading, listening, and watching thought leaders in the business field. The culture is changing all the time, and it's important to stay current and informed.

Recommended Reading

Atlas of the Heart, Brené Brown

Dare to Lead, Brené Brown

The Gifts of Imperfection, Brené Brown

First, Break All the Rules, Marcus Buckingham

Love + Work, Marcus Buckingham

The 5 Languages of Appreciation in the Workplace, Gary Chapman and Paul White

BE 2.0, Jim Collins

Good to Great, Jim Collins

Smart Tribes, Christine Comaford

The Culture Code, Daniel Coyle

The Talent Code, Daniel Coyle

Grit, Angela Duckworth

Tribes, Seth Godin

Think Again, Adam Grant

The B Corp Handbook, Ryan Honeyman

How to Be an Antiracist, Ibram X. Kendi

Four Obsessions of an Extraordinary Executive, Patrick Lencioni

The Sum of Us, Heather McGhee

The Primes, Chris McGoff

Crucial Conversations, Kerry Patterson et al.

Drive, Daniel H. Pink

To Sell is Human, Daniel H. Pink

When, Daniel H. Pink

Start with Why, Simon Sinek

Leaders Eat Last, Simon Sinek

The Gap and the Gain, Dan Sullivan

Never Split the Difference, Christopher Voss and Tahl Raz

Traction, Gino Wickman

How to be a Great Boss, Gino Wickman and René Boer

ABOUT THE AUTHOR

NANCY J. GEENEN is the visionary and CEO of Flexability, recognized for three consecutive years as a "Best for the World: Governance" by B Labs. In 2022, Inc. recognized Flexability as Best in Business for Management Consulting. Nancy drives the culture and strategy of this social impact workplace consulting firm, building high-performance teams through diversity, equity, and inclusion in the workplace. She believes that company culture drives growth and profitability. Nancy is known for her ability to simplify the complex in her strategy and scenario planning work, skills that served her well in managing risk in "bet the company" trials. Nancy leads by example, with an exploratory mindset that creates opportunity for idea exchange and development of best practices in ESG, CSR, and DEI.

As a business leader, Nancy brings process and governance to every organization with which she works. As the office managing partner for the Northern California offices of a global law firm, she successfully restructured the offices to profitability, increased revenue, and opened new offices, during which time the *San Francisco Business Times* named the San Francisco office one of its Best Places to Work and named Nancy as one of the Most Influential Women in Bay Area Business for eight consecutive years, including the first class of its hall of fame. Subsequently, Nancy founded and managed a trial consulting firm. She grew that organization to $6 million in revenue in less than four years, after which she sold her equity position. Nancy served for two years as the interim CEO for a $30 million self-sustaining 501(c)(3) focused on employment of individuals with disabilities. Based on her experience with the nonprofit, Nancy founded Flexability with several members of the nonprofit executive team.

Nancy is a graduate of Harvard Business School - OPM 50 and the Harvard VPAL Cybersecurity Managing Risk in the Information Age program. She holds a JD from Santa Clara University School of Law and an MA in education and a BA in English from Stanford University while earning varsity letters in three sports. Nancy is licensed to practice in California and the District of Columbia. She serves as a panelist at the MassTLC Board Ready Bootcamp and as a guest lecturer in the Wisconsin School of Business at the University of Wisconsin–Madison.

Nancy has a passion for helping other entrepreneurs and their leadership teams develop the skills they need to strengthen the business and achieve their long-term goals. She continues to work with business owners focused on growth and stakeholder primacy. For Nancy, workplace inclusion is a philosophy and the future of work. Championing people results in better productivity and drives financial and social well-being. Nancy is a certified advanced facilitator, Professional EOS Implementer, and Predictive Index Certified Partner for talent optimization.

Visit www.nancygeenen.com to read her blogs. She can be reached by email at info@nancygeenen.com or on LinkedIn @njgeenen. For more information about Flexability, visit the website at www.flexability.com.